SHAKE OFF THE SNAKE

MAKING THE SHIFT FROM WEARIER TO WARRIOR

A.J. Rubano, D.C.

"But Paul shook the snake off into
the fire and suffered no ill effects."
Acts 28:5

Outskirts Press, Inc.
Denver, Colorado

This book is dedicated to my Lord and Savior Jesus Christ.

Title page scriptural reference is from the
New International Version of the Bible; all other
scripture references, unless otherwise noted, are from
the King James Version of the Bible.

ACKNOWLEDGEMENTS

Thank you to Pastor David T. Demola, my father in the faith for all your encouragement and Godly example. Your teaching and preaching has been a resounding reminder of what God can and will do in my life. Thank you to Pastors John Antonucci and Joe Fortunato for your fire and friendship. Thank you to Charles Grevious, John Banks, David Clarke and David Gall for your continuing prayers and support. Thanks Tom Kanell for your input and insight. Thank you to the following teachers of the word for their willingness to share their lives and experiences: Rev. Richard Tedesco, Rev. Rosemary Manthey, Rev Joe Balina, Rev. David Sellers, Rev. Anthony Spero, Rev. Al Moreno, Rev. Cedric Miller, Bishop Moss, and Mother Cuthpert Thank you to Rev. Daniel Pena for your inspiration and love.

Thank you to Kay Clarke for her input and expertise in the cover design, and for being a fantastic sister-in-law.

Thanks Mom and Dad for always instilling in me the faith to believe I can accomplish anything I put my mind to and for your many sacrifices to give me the opportunities to succeed. Thank you to my brother Ryan, I am proud of the father you have become and for the beautiful nephews and niece you and Tina have given our family. Thank you Kyra, Philip, and Kayla for being the best children a dad can hope for. Thank you to Patricia Baker for your support and for bringing my best friend, your daughter, into the world at just the right time for us to meet.

Thanks especially to my wife, Sonia, for her love, support, and patience with me through all the storms and snakes that life can bring

TABLE OF CONTENTS

FOREWORD

More than ever before, we need to know what we believe and why we believe it. We live in a day and age where Satan knows that his time is short and will do everything in his power to deceive and ensnare the body of Christ. He has a plethora of traps, schemes and devices planned to stop you from experiencing everything Jesus Christ came to give you. The enemy works tirelessly to discourage you and to cause you to faint in your mind and give up. We first encounter him in the Garden of Eden where he appeared as a serpent and beguiled Eve. He was able to inflict his poisonous venom of deception that caused them to lose everything that God had provided for them. The Bible clearly tells us in James 4:7 that we are to submit ourselves unto God, resist the devil, and he will flee from us. In Dr. AJ Rubano's book "Shake off the Snake" you will receive a clear understanding of Satan's plans and devices meant to take you down. Dr. Rubano outlines the different types of venom the enemy uses today to neutralize the believer and keep them from a victorious life in Christ. You will receive practical insight on "how to" avoid the snake bite and what to do when he fastens himself upon you.

Vipers don't just attack people for no reason, they attack when you make a conscious decision to advance into their territory. The Apostle Paul was moving sticks into the fire to cause it to burn brighter. Every time you make a decision to build the kingdom of God you experience more of God's fire in your life. The enemy doesn't want you to experience God's fire, he would much rather you experience religion. Many of God's people have been snake bit and are starting to see the diabolical results of the poison that has been injected. Though the snake has infected many people with discouragement, doubt, fear, worry, anger, unforgiveness and bitterness we have to remember that when he bites it is primarily with the intent to get you and me to pull back from the fire of God. The typical first reaction to a snake bite is to pull your hand back. Isn't it interesting to note that when we are bitten by the enemy of our souls that is just the reaction he is hoping to see manifested. He wants you to pull back from going to church and serving God. He wants you to pull back on your giving. He wants you to become complacent so you stop being hot for the things of God. If he can get you to pull back his venom has been effective. Paul didn't have the reaction most of us would have had. He didn't move his hand from the fire because he knew the only way to defeat his enemy was to shake him right off in the midst of the fire. "Shake off the Snake" will show you how to stay right in the fire of God and defeat the enemy that has been trying to defeat you! When you learn to shake him off you will see that his venom will not produce the effect he was after but push you closer into God's arms and the destiny he has for your life.

Pastor John Antonucci
Faith Fellowship World Outreach Ministries
Fort Myers, Florida

INTRODUCTION

Perhaps nothing is more representative of fear than a slithering, hissing snake. As prevalent as the thoughts brought on by snakes is the destructive power of fear brought on by adverse situations in our day to day lives. Never before has there been such a prevailing spirit of anxiety, discouragement, and depression. And it seems that now more than ever the body of Christ needs a word of encouragement to bring victory over the foes that set believers back and keep them from their divine destiny.

Saint Patrick, the most beloved and popular of all Irish Saints is credited with driving snakes from Ireland. As legend would have it Saint Patrick is said to have filled all the Emerald Isle with shamrocks so that the snakes would never return, and indeed today there are no species of snakes inhabiting the island.

Just as snakes in the real world have different styles of defending themselves and attacking their prey; and come in varying colors and lengths the "snakes" in your life will take many forms. Some are real, while others are merely a figment of your imagination brought about by fear. They can be the embodiment of both spiritual and psychological disturbance, but in every case they can and do exert a tangible impact on our way of thinking, feeling, and acting. The "snake" can be an actual personification of the devil as well as the roadblocks to your success in life. It can be the result of an all out attack brought on by the enemy of your soul or the consequences of self induced poisonous habits, attitudes and mindsets that adversely control your destiny. While diverse in appearance one thing is certain; if we are to fulfill the plans God has for our life than the presence of the snake must be conquered.

History makes it seem a certainty that it was not actual snake species that were removed by Saint Patrick (since that most likely happened during some ice age), but rather the demonic influences and evil spirits that resided in the country at that time. It was his stance against pagan influence and his ability to convert the heathen to Christianity that shook up the spiritual tenor of the land.

In writing this book that has been my overriding motivation: to shake up the body of Christ so that they can shake off the effects of the snake. For those battling frustration over failed dreams, fear about what the future holds, and brought down by depression this is a guide to getting your spiritual "groove" back. For those who haven't lost their confidence in the Almighty, but have been, themselves shaken by the feelings of distress all around them it's a wake up call to stoke up the flames and press in even more deeply to their Father.

Make no mistake about it, Satan wants to "sift you, and the church as a whole, as wheat", and if he can't do it himself he wants to cause you to do it yourself. He'd like nothing better than to cause you to commit spiritual suicide. He wants to knock out your ability to dream and dream big. Rest assured, your heavenly daddy has already made the way out for you...*if* you can trust HIM and take HIM at HIS word.

As you apply the godly principles detailed in the pages ahead you will find that not only are you able to overcome the attacks the enemy has set for you, but you will actually learn how to benefit from them, as they become your stepping stones to success. Literally your weakest areas will become your strongest as you determine to shake off the snake and let God help you take everything the snakes in your life have meant for harm and use them for good.

Be confident that God is on your side as you attempt to draw closer to Him and fulfill your destiny. He wants you to succeed. Don't believe anyone who tells you your heavenly father is bringing something in your life with the intent to punish you or make your life difficult. Nothing could be further from the truth. As Jesus said powerfully in Matthew 7:9-11, **"Or what man is there of you, whom if his son ask bread, will give him a stone? Or if he ask a fish, will give him a serpent? If ye then, being evil, give good gifts unto your children how much more shall your father which is in heaven give good things to them that ask him?"** He didn't put the serpent in your path, but you can rest assured when you mean business he will help you Shake Off the Snake.

"ONCE BITTEN BY A SNAKE,
HE IS SCARED ALL
HIS LIFE AT THE MERE
SIGHT OF A ROPE."

CHINESE PROVERB

CHAPTER 1

FEAR OF SNAKES

Fear is only as deep as the mind allows.

-- Japanese Proverb.

I don't know about you but just about everyone I have talked to and know, with rare exception, has a general disdain or hatred of snakes. I am not talking about the likes of the late Steve Irwins of this world or other reptile lovers who not only like snakes but actually go in search of them. I can tell you in all honesty you will never catch me walking barefoot along the Amazon just hoping for a chance to step on a "beautiful" anaconda or boa constrictor,

Definitely, not gonna happen.

In general snakes just aren't high on the list when most people talk about pet ownership. Maybe it is the way they wriggle along the ground or the thought of them lunging out fangs flaring. Perhaps it's that forked tongue that juts out incessantly, or the "sneakiness" as a curled up snake hides in the bushes. Or just maybe the thought of a slimy moist snake crossing over your feet or along your arms or

1

legs is enough to just give you the creeps.

Why else would just about every episode of Fear Factor involve snakes in a box that some unlucky contestant is going to have to come in contact with to win a measly $100,000.

For me, I think it started with a biology class in junior high school of all places. My instructor was a kind enough middle aged woman who looked somewhat younger than her actual age, I am sure. Her goal was to gain our attention and develop an appreciation and respect for science and nature. She started out much the same way most teachers begin the school year, or at least what I felt was the normal way, by having each student introduce themselves to the rest of their classmates (an exercise we had all grown bored with since we had done it about five times already that day). She then proceeded to tell us about herself, how long she had been teaching, how many children she had, and of course how much she enjoyed teaching science.

A Shuddering Thought

She then walked over to a tank containing two Ball Pythons, named such because they have a habit of curling into a ball. She pulled one of the snakes out, I am not sure if it was a female or male, and allowed the snake to wrap itself around her arm. After observing the reactions of our class she made the offer you knew was inevitable, "Who would like to hold the snake?" I still can picture when this one young man held the snake, he wanted to be the first to conquer his fear, so he boldly stepped up, raised his hand and offered to be the first guinea pig, while the rest of us feared he might be the last for all the wrong reasons. As he reached out his arm to hold the reptile you could see he was

SHAKE OFF THE SNAKE

visibly shaking, unfamiliar with this kind of thing so he took a deep breath as our teacher encouraged and calmed him by reassuring him this snake had never attacked anyone.

And then it happened...

Absolutely nothing! The snake curled on his arm but other than that not a thing. After everyone saw how smoothly things went for snake handler number one we began to line up for our chance to overcome our own fears. Some of the girls put the snake around their necks, all under the watchful eye of the teacher of course, while most people were content to just let the snake crawl around their arms. I was next in line when the snake went crazy. For some unknown reason it decided to take a swipe at the young girl holding him and pricked the skin near her shoulder, she was terrified, and needless to say the snake holding exercise was discontinued.

Why was this different?

The Mind's Eye Takes Lasting Photos

Now, I've been chased by dogs, bitten by a dog, and even kicked by a horse but for some reason witnessing this snake bite sent a chill through me I had never experienced. It left an indelible impression that visually repeated itself within my mind's eye over and over again, triggered by anything remotely related to a snake.

Perhaps you've experienced something similar in your life that had the same kind of impact. Something that sent such a profound shock wave through you that you can still see it if you close your eyes and think; something that has prevented you from pursuing your dreams, goals, and ambitions. Something that sent you spiraling away from your destiny and purpose or worse yet, has kept you from believing in your God-given skills and talents and has paralyzed you with a fear that has gripped you, stifling growth.

Those closest to you may not even know, they may suspect something is off, but they don't really know or understand the internal emotions that drive this very real perception that has invaded your whole thought process.

Maybe it was an exact moment or instance that began the domino effect, or perhaps it was a series of poor choices. But whether it was an obvious event or a subtle, slow to come about process the snake reared its ugly head back and latched on.

In my years in chiropractic practice I have seen these very real fears sap the life out of people. Seemingly minor events on the surface imposed a heavy emotional, and consequently, a drastic outward physical toll as well. Were the fears warranted? After all in nearly every instance the people never came close to experiencing the same tragic events again in real life. But you had better believe they felt them happen over and over again in their minds eye. Can a rope pose a threat? Were the fears real? They were real to them. And that was all that mattered.

More importantly though is the fact that the power to overcome those fears, the right to deal with them on their own terms and not have those terms dictated to them by some external force was theirs for the taking. I found the best and most effective way to handle fear is to face it head on, to deal with the source of the issue.

One of the underlying philosophies of my profession is to treat causes not symptoms. Instead of just focusing on pain we look for the source of the pain because very often if pain is removed before the problem is dealt with the protective mechanism is gone and the source of the malfunction will actually worsen in its absence.

If you have struggled with fear, wondering how the enemy, the snake is going to have his way with you, what he is going to do next to make your life miserable you don't have to remain in that position. You have the choice to make to be free. Much like the patients I treat on a daily basis, who have a choice between addressing symptoms or treating causes yes their may be a little pain in the beginning, but ultimately, when they choose to follow my recommendations and make some lifestyle changes they get the results they are looking for. Is it a quick fix? Sometimes yes; but usually it is a process that starts with a first step.

Another Night with the Frogs

I learned something watching the animated film "The Prince of Egypt" with my children that has helped me help many of the people who seek my advice. A critical scene in the movie involved a confrontation between the Egyptian Pharaoh and the former Prince of Egypt, Moses. The two had been brothers and experienced a very fierce sibling rivalry as depicted in the beginning of the movie, battling for the approval and affirmation of their father. In the scene of which I am referring Moses returned to Egypt after spending years in the desert, on the run from his past and trying to run from his destiny as the deliverer for his people, the Israelites who were enslaved under Egyptian rule.

As Moses came before the Pharaoh it was clear that the years of rivalry were still engraved in the young Pharaoh's memory, and he was certainly not about to be trumped by his one time adversary and "imposter" to the throne of Egypt. So as Moses came to him to ask for the release of his people Ramses refused. With each refusal came a plague meant to break one of the symbols of Egyptian strength; economic, religious, or political.

One such plague was rather interesting and I know most certainly would have caught my attention very quickly. It was the plague of the Frogs. After yet another refusal by Pharaoh to let the Israelites go and pursue freedom a plethora of frogs invaded every area of Egyptian life.

Imagine waking to find you had frogs in your bedroom and bathroom, thousands of frogs in your garage, croaking frogs in your underwear drawer. How about frogs in your pantry closet, under your sheets, and in your child's crib?

I don't even like it when there are a few frogs stuck to my windows after a rain storm. Due to this plague frogs were not just on the windows, they were on the roof, in the gutters, in the pool, hopping around the living room, sticking to the side of the refrigerator and stove. Frogs would have been coming out of the microwave, bounding from the hamper, or swirling around the washing machine: literally frogs in every nook and cranny of the house.

The curious thing to this whole frog ordeal was not so much that it was yet another plague, but Pharaoh's response. Moses asked Pharaoh a very pointed and very deliberate question, as he had done with each of the other plagues. He asked "When should I ask God to stop this frog invasion." Whatever Pharaoh answered Moses was prepared to do. So what does Pharaoh say in response. "Tomorrow!" Not today, not right now, not this second, tomorrow! With just a few cockroaches in my house I'd be calling Orkin and saying get over here right away, and yet for something so severe, so disgusting, he says tomorrow. I

SHAKE OFF THE SNAKE

don't know what the Pharaoh was thinking, maybe he thought his magician's could do something about it, maybe he went into his "man cave" and was trying to figure it out, or maybe he thought they would just hop out of there on their own. Maybe he just wanted to "think it over" for a few hours. Whatever the reason, he decided to spend one more night with the frogs.

Let me ask you this. What is your reason for spending one more day living less than your best? Why are you still hobbling around an emotional cripple? How long will you continue to squirm in your chair or bed because you are worried about what tomorrow holds? What is keeping you from letting go of your problem and breaking the cycle of physical, emotional, or mental pain?

One of the questions I always ask a patient before starting a treatment plan is "when would you like to get started." You'd be amazed at how often I hear next week, next month, or after I get settled in my new job. If it was me and I had just been handed the keys to a new me, there is no way I'd hesitate, I wouldn't want to wait another day. I'd want to get started right away. I wouldn't spend one more night dealing with the frog. I wouldn't allow the serpent one more day to torment me. When are *YOU* ready to get started? I know what I'd say......

Well now is the time and what you will read and put into practice over the course of this work has in it the power to deliver you and free you from years, even decades of bondage. All you've got to do is be willing to SHAKE OFF THE SNAKE.

"WE WERE GRANTED THE RIGHT
TO NAME THE THINGS AND PEOPLE
WE EITHER HAVE OWNERSHIP OF
OR HAVE BEEN GIVEN AUTHORITY OVER."

"ADAM BLAMED EVE, EVE BLAMED
THE SERPENT AND THE SERPENT
DIDN'T HAVE A LEG TO STAND ON."

UNKNOWN

CHAPTER 2

WHO'S AFRAID OF
THE BIG BAD SNAKE?

You can delegate authority, but not responsibility.

Stephen W. Comiskey

N ow the serpent was more subtil than any beast of the field which the LORD God had made. And he said unto the woman, Yea, hath God said, Ye shall not eat of every tree of the garden? And the woman said unto the serpent, We may eat of the fruit of the trees of the garden: But of the fruit of the tree which is in the midst of the garden, God hath said, Ye shall not eat of it, neither shall ye touch it, lest ye die. **Genesis 3:1-3**

God's people weren't always afraid of snakes. In the Garden of Eden Adam and Eve walked around in peace, not fearing any of the creatures in their midst. As I read the scripture I see them commanding the animals they were in charge of naming. As the lion and bear walked by Adam spoke over it the name that seemed fitting to him and

"LION" and "BEAR" came out, the same with the monkey, and sea turtle, and yes, the serpent.

Name it and Claim it!

You don't naturally fear the things you are called on naming, do you. In my life the first thing I named was a parakeet, I called him "SWAT" after one of the television shows I watched. I later named a dog (Josh), a rabbit (Mary), a car (the FET mobile, don't ask), and my children (Kyra, Philip, and Kayla). I learned early on in my life, under the teaching of men and women that carried a fear in their hearts for the Lord that I needed to choose names that lined up with the results we wanted to see. So, I named my business Accurate because I wanted it to be so, especially since we care for people's health. I doubt anyone would want to go to Careless Chiropractic (although the alliteration sounds cool). My wife and I gave all of our children the middle name Daniel(lle) because it means "God is my Judge" and we want them to spend their lives living for Him.

We were granted the right to name the things and people we either have ownership of or have been given authority over. In functional homes, parents don't fear their children it's the other way around. The parent is in the position of authority to train up that child so that as he or she grows up they learn the things that will enable them to have good lives. I know some have taken this to the wrong degree and have abused their role, but the truth of the matter is that part of the task in parenting is to lead and direct, and this must be done with authority. It is the parent who has had the life experiences and training to know what is good and what is harmful; so that when a child comes in off the street and says "so and so said that such and such is ok" the parent can lovingly say "yes" or "no" depending upon what is in the best interest of the child. The same is true in a business ownership position. Although a business owner may have trusted employees who he has hired to help with a part of the business he still has the final say and needs to know what the best direction of the company is. In my business I have outside consultants and advisors who make suggestions that I as an entrepreneur need to investigate carefully. Every decision I make affects my ability to stay afloat and also puts my reputation and license on the line. Let me give you a clear example.

Who is in Charge?

One of the first patients I had visit me in my clinic was an elderly woman who came in to see me for pain in her lower back. She was a very sweet grandma type, but her husband was somewhat of a pit bull. They had relocated to Florida from the Northeast where the husband had been very successful as an executive for a large manufacturing firm. Needless to say he was used to commanding his team of workers and sales people, and having them do what he said. To top it off he was a little upset at the treatment his wife had been provided at a nearby hospital so he was not in a pleasant mood.

As this couple entered my office I could see from the look on the wife's face that she was in a lot of discomfort, and I could see from the look on the husband's face that he wanted action. It did not surprise me one bit that he came in and nearly chewed off the head of one of my secretaries. Fortunately for this man she is a sweet young lady who understands that hurting people often hurt people, so she put up very calmly with his crass demeanor, and filled me in on what she experienced as she brought the couple back into my examination room. I was prepared.

As I walked in and greeted them, as is always my custom to get to know people as people, not patients, he started right in. "You need to get my wife better now. We had a Chiropractor up north and he would just manipulate her spine and she would be fine" he barked. As he was about to continue on, I had already heard enough. I quickly reminded him that he was in MY office, that I was the expert, and that I would be happy to do whatever it took to help his wife BUT I would do it my way or he was free to take her someplace else. I looked at the wife and said "You want to get better, don't you", she nodded yes. The husband calmed down momentarily, I believe startled that I had the audacity to address him as I had.

I began my process of collecting information and conducted a brief examination after which I recommended we take x-rays of her back. The husband was livid. "What do you mean you want to take x-rays, she has been going to the chiropractor for years and all he does is put her on her side and manipulate her spine. Why can't *you* do that, *he* never took any x-rays." Right there I could have backed down and said "yes, Mr. Patient you are right I don't need to take any x-rays", but if I did I wouldn't have been doing my job properly. I was the expert, I was the one with the legal authority to determine what I allowed in my business. One more time I looked this man in the face, and this time lovingly, yet firmly I asserted "You are free to take your wife to another office where they may choose to do an adjustment on her without x-rays, in fact I'll be glad to give you the name of a couple who actually might, but if she is going to be treated here I am going to do x-rays." I also told him I thought if she had treatment elsewhere without x-rays it would be a BIG mistake.

The end result? He relented and I took the x-rays *and* found two fractures in her spine. Had I treated her with traditional chiropractic care she most certainly would have walked out worse than she came in and perhaps may have sued me at a later time. That is what ownership and authority is all about. And when you name something you either have ownership or authority over it.

I named my clinic Accurate Chiropractic, and fortunately for someone's grand-mother I took the time and recognized my authority to be true to that name. By the way, I never actually treated this woman, because of the fractures I sent her to a specialist who was able to get her better. To this day, though, she and her husband are two of my "raving fans" and have told most of their friends with back problems about me.

Authority over Snakes

The Bible tells us *we have been given power to tread on serpents and scorpions and over all the power of the enemy, and nothing shall by any means hurt us* (Luke 10:19). That is the same power that the first man and woman had.

Eve wasn't afraid of the serpent, remember her husband Adam had been given the role of naming all the living things by God, himself (Genesis 2:19). Furthermore, you don't hold a casual conversation with something you are afraid of. So in the cool of the day Eve walks by the Tree of the Knowledge of Good and Evil and has a little talk with one of the "little" earth creatures only she doesn't realize that Satan had entered into the serpent and was out to beguile her.

What happens next is where mankind gets off the train.

Not just in the sense of disobedience to God that resulted in being kicked out of the Garden, but also in the area of fear. *They* now experienced fear for the first time; fearing God not as the father HE is, but as someone who wanted to punish them. They looked at themselves and were ashamed of their nakedness.

All because they failed to recognize their inheritance, and the truth of God's word. Look again at the end of the conversation Eve had with the serpent…

And the woman said unto the serpent, We may eat of the fruit of the trees of the garden: But of the fruit of the tree which is in the midst of the garden, God hath said, <u>Ye shall not eat of it, neither shall ye touch it</u>, lest ye die. Genesis 3:2-3

A careful study of the word shows she missed out on what God *really* said about the tree

And the LORD God commanded the man, "You are free to eat from any tree in the garden; but you must not eat from the tree of the knowledge of good and evil, for when <u>you eat of it</u> you will surely die." Genesis 2:16-17

Eve added to the words that God had spoken making it look as if He just wanted to spoil her fun, she listened to the voice of Satan embodied in the serpent, she ate of the fruit, shared it with her man and then she and Adam took turns passing the responsibility onto God Himself and the rest is history. Or is it? What follows next is the result of NOT knowing one's position of authority and dominion. It did not and does not have to be that way. Adam and Eve missed the mark, true, but their biggest error, the one that sealed their fate was not eating the fruit of the tree but failing to recognize their responsibility and repenting to the Father.

ACTIVELY COMMITTING SIN IS DAMAGING AND HAS ITS CONSEQUENCES; FAILING TO FACE UP TO IT PUTS US IN THE POSITION OF FEAR, GUILT, SHAME, AND CONDEMNATION.

It was the error of omission, not commission that sentenced them to life outside of paradise. It is the same error that dogs believers today. Actively committing sin is damaging and has its consequences; failing to face up to it puts us in the position of fear, guilt, shame, and condemnation. It is a place men have struggled with since the fall.

Confront and Commit

If we are to overcome the snake in our life it is essential we confront the sins we commit and commit to defeating the hold sinful activities have in our lives. Nothing will inhibit your ability to defeat the snake in your life more than your own sin.

Let me see if I can bring this concept home for you with an example from my field of practice. Most people are familiar with the joke about the man who complains to his doctor that he gets pain when he lifts his arm and the doctor responds by telling him "don't do that" and writes out a bill for $200.

Humorous as it may sound there are many instances

where the obvious remedy is plain to everyone except for the one suffering with the problem. I see this on an every day basis in my practice. People want the quick fix and want to pay as little as possible for that fix to boot. Unless I can convey to the members of my practice the role they play in maintaining good health and preventing injury I fail to live up to the standards of ethical practice.

Therefore, in addition to making spinal adjustments and administering exercise programs and therapies to correct joint and muscle dysfunction I also am compelled to make lifestyle recommendations to reduce the need for my services.

Imagine for a moment if I recognized that a patient, we'll call her Mrs. Smith, had a neck problem that was so severe it often kept her from going to work, caused migraine headaches, and prevented her from spending quality time with her children responded well to my treatment yet had to return on a regular basis because her problem continually resurfaced.

As part of my professional duty I would need to investigate further the cause of her repeating exacerbations of her condition. In other words it would be my job to identify what it is that prevents her from realizing complete deliverance from her condition. To do that would require her to honestly answer some questions about her lifestyle and activities; as well as some observation on my part with a trained eye to determine if there was anything she overlooked.

Now let's say between the two of us we were able to determine that the main reason for her frequent head and neck symptoms was the fact that she stayed up late every night eating a tub of ice cream and watching television with her head propped up on several pillows and scrunched into her chest.

SHAKE OFF THE SNAKE

In this case my recommendations would be fairly simple. Cut out the tub of ice cream and watch television while *sitting up* for a few less hours. The problem will go away permanently and by doing so would allow her to make more income due to less time lost at work, be friendlier to her husband since she no longer experienced the headaches, and spend more quality time with her children.

At this point Mrs. Smith has the choice to make. She can continue to see me three times per week to treat the pain or she can decide to follow the prescription that has been shown to bring total resolution of her issue time and time again.

Now she may not want to follow my advice, and that is up to her, but if she wants to enjoy the things she has defined to me as important family and work responsibilities it may mean putting aside something that is seemingly enjoyable but is truly costly for something much more productive and lasting.

If you are going to shake off the snake you are going to have to develop a little bit of a doctor's mindset. Investigate your ways. Take an introspective look at your lifestyle so that you can identify areas under your direct control that will enable you to be the person you have been called to be and do the things you have been called to do. Know this; you can't just confess away everything in your life. As much as I would like to rebuke the calories in the foods I eat and confess that poor eating habits won't make me fat I am subject to the laws God put in place when he created this earth. Even though Mrs. Smith may want to deny that her television watching habits are not affecting her neck the facts say otherwise and unless she takes proactive steps to address the cause she will have to take continued reactive steps to the effects. If you know there are snakes in certain bushes stay away from those bushes. There are times, and this qualifies as one of them when you have to do something to help your situation and naturally reinforce what God is doing in the supernatural.

And don't worry you will not have to do this alone. You can get help from trained eyes, from the godly men and women in your life, and from the Holy Spirit. I am reminded of what we are taught in Psalm 139: 22-24.

Search me, O God, and know my heart: try me, and know my thoughts: And see if there be any wicked way in me, and lead me in the way everlasting.

God knows you better than you know yourself so open your ears and listen to *His* voice. Receive His instruction so that you can identify and remedy the sin in your life and increase your ability to overcome the snake's attack on your destiny.

Fiery Serpents

And the people spake against God, and against Moses, Wherefore have ye brought us up out of Egypt to die in the wilderness? For there is no bread, neither is there any water; and our soul loatheth this light bread. And the LORD sent fiery serpents among the people, and they bit the people; and much people of Israel died. Numbers 21:5-6

The children of Israel had been delivered from the hard hand of Egyptian rule. They were slaves and had been sorely dealt with in Egypt; they cried out for deliverance and received it in the most miraculous of ways. God demonstrated his awesome power over the false gods the Egyptians worshipped, over Pharaoh, and over the most powerful nation of that time. The plagues that are recorded in the Book of Exodus were not just meant to end the physical enslavement of the Israelites, but also to symbolize that Jehovah is the final authority, the one true God. As we discussed earlier a study of these plagues shows that they affected the economic center of Egyptian life (the Nile River), the gods of fertility, the sun god, and the supposed wise men (magicians) of that region.

And Moses and Aaron went in unto Pharaoh, and they did so as the LORD had commanded: and Aaron cast down his rod before Pharaoh, and before his servants, and it became a serpent. Then Pharaoh also called the wise men and the sorcerers: now the magicians of Egypt, they also did in like manner with their enchantments. For they cast down every man his rod, and they became serpents: but Aaron's rod swallowed up their rods. Exodus 7:10-12

Needless to say, after watching the rod of God swallow up the magicians' rods, the children of Israel had a clear demonstration of *the* Almighty One!

Unfortunately, the impression this left on them was not long lived. By the time we catch up to them in the passage recorded in Numbers chapter twenty-one they have become incessant moaners and complainers. They whine to Moses about the food they receive, they complain about their water, they say they have had enough and basically want to go back to Egypt. They would rather work for the man who made them make bricks without straw and have nothing to call their own than obey the Lord. God in all his mercy and grace put up with this.

Continuing the Blame Game

Where the Israelites went wrong, again, was in playing the blame game. Just like Adam and Eve they didn't take responsibility for their actions, they put it on someone else. It really didn't matter who was to blame, as long as it wasn't them. The scripture tells us "they spake against God and Moses." They never once looked in the mirror and asked, "Where did I go wrong", they never wondered if they missed the mark. Instead they "loathed" what God *did* provide for them. They didn't need to work, just follow and obey, and they couldn't do that.

Listen to this, if you do it will change your life. People always say they want the easy life, but presented with the "easy" life *these* people couldn't stand it, it wasn't enough for them. If you want everything easy you will only just get by in life, barely scraping along.

It reminds me of the sports teams that continually play to the level of their opponent. They disappoint their fans because when they play a solid opponent they play really well, just not well enough to win. When they are pitted against a weak team they play very poor and either barely scrape out a victory or find a way to lose to a team that never should have beaten them.

This method will only keep you right where you are. If you are ever going to fulfill your dreams, get the "easy" life concept out of your head. Set your gaze on the prize, whatever it is and go for it full throttle with the guidance of the Holy Spirit, and the power of God behind you.

Where's The Gratitude?

Second, if you fail to recognize what has been provided

to you and for you, you cannot reasonably expect to receive more. Can you imagine the audacity of the Israelites complaining about the manna sent to them from heaven for their daily meals? Manna is translated as "what is it". It could have been anything the Israelites wanted it to be; lobster, steak, even an ice cream sundae. It could have been a full course meal each and every day, and yet all they could see it for was "light bread."

It kind of reminds me of something from my childhood. I remember as clear as it were yesterday how we dealt with financial hardship in our home. My brother Ryan and I would beg to go out to a restaurant with my mom and dad, not realizing the cost of things and the responsibilities our folks were dealing with we thought it a small thing. What did my mom do to help us overcome the fact we couldn't afford to go out to eat? She had us make signs and menus and pretend. We made signs for everything from McDonald's to Sizzler and Red Lobster; and then we would take turns serving each other dressed like the waiters and waitresses from these fine eating establishments. To me and my brother it made dinnertime fun and we enjoyed the food and the game probably more than we would have appreciated the restaurant. Little did I know my mom and dad were teaching me what faith was all about. They taught us to take what we had with gratitude, to be pleased with what we had and also to dream big.

The Israelites didn't even have to go this far, just enjoy what they had and focus on the blessing of "what is it" that God provided every day. No, if you can't be thankful for what you *have* you disqualify yourself from receiving the future blessings that God has for you.

The Israelites found themselves in a predicament again after failing to accept responsibility and taking for granted the gift of God in their lives. This time it was their own doing and they faced the fiery serpents and many died.

"ONE THING YOU NEED TO KNOW, HOWEVER, IS THAT A SNAKE IN THE NATURAL WILL NOT SWALLOW SOMETHING THAT IS BIGGER THAN THE DIAMETER AT ITS WIDEST PART AND EVEN IF IT DID IT WOULD LITERALLY KILL HIM."

"THE COMPETITION WILL BITE YOU IF YOU KEEP RUNNING, IF YOU STAND STILL, THEY WILL SWALLOW YOU."

VICTOR KIAM

CHAPTER 3

DON'T BE SWALLOWED WHOLE

*"A communist is like a crocodile: when it opens its
mouth you cannot tell whether it is trying to
smile or preparing to eat you up."*

Winston Churchill

Picture this scene from a fraternity party. Five frat brothers standing around a keg of beer, one says to another "betcha I can swallow three goldfish.... *whole*." With the other frat brothers looking on he psyches himself up, as they chant "Go, Go, Go", he reaches into the fish bowl grabs an unsuspecting gold fish by the tail and lowers it, past his lips past the base of his tongue and....gulp.....swallows it *whole*.

There are species of slithering serpents that get their nutrition the same way, literally swallowing their prey in one gulp and then using their powerful muscles to push their meal along the digestive tract. In fact for most non venomous snakes this is the method of choice. And they will use this method whether their prey is dead or alive.

The enemy of our soul is no different. If he sees you can't be poisoned, he can't get you to go after the forbidden fruits and traps he's laid for you, he will seek other methods of reducing your threat to his kingdom. He's already tried to get you to chase after pornography, when you've been away from home on business or on the internet late at night sending pop ups to try to trip you up. But no... you stood by the word and would not be dissuaded. He's tried to infect your thinking with regard to the leadership of your church, but you would not lift your voice against God's anointed. Even efforts to poison you against your brothers and sisters in the Lord have been unsuccessful as you chose not to lower yourself to gossiping, but instead esteeming those around you even more than yourself.

An Inside Job

The enemy has been trying to get to know you. The word tells us "but the serpent was craftier.." (Genesis 3:1)The last thing Satan wants to see you do is fulfill your God given potential, your journey, and your progression that your Lord has planned for you. So what does he do, he observes. He watches for a time of weakness or inattentiveness. And then he strikes....

In the movie "Donnie Brasco", starring Al Pacino and Johnny Depp, Depp played the part of an FBI agent who went under cover as a mobster. His job was to infiltrate the mafia to gain the confidence of the big bosses, and to give inside information to the FBI so that they could successfully anticipate the organizations next move of large scale drug trafficking. Although a fictional story it illustrates a tactic used by the government and illegal criminal organizations alike. To stop a criminal you almost have to think like one. To subvert the authorities the criminal mind seeks to understand and avoid the pre-emptive strategies of law enforcement.

Even seemingly harmless snakes, like the common garter snake, use this same tactic. They observe their prey before first swallowing, then suffocating, then digesting their prey.

Stay On Guard

"Be sober, be vigilant for your enemy walks about like a roaring lion, seeking whom he may devour" 1 Peter 5:8

If you are not careful he will use this tactic on you. No, you won't physically be swallowed and suffocated, but your dreams and hopes for the future will be devoured. Think about it, how did you respond the last time you had a financial set back? Did it stop you from trusting in God's ability to provide for you, even a little? Did it prevent you from taking a risk that may have catapulted your finances? Did it cause you to lower your expectations or vision for the future? Did it get you off course for a period of weeks, months, or even years? Or how about this one, did it have the effect of stopping you from sowing into the kingdom?

What about your health? Perhaps you were sailing along in good condition, even undertaking an exercise program and eating healthy when you were derailed by an illness of some sort. Did you stop believing that God is Jehovah Raphe? (The Lord your Healer) Perhaps, he is the healer for every one else, just not me?

I've found out that this doesn't just happen once, but can occur periodically throughout our lives at different stages and levels. We need to be diligent to guard our hearts during periods of transition in our lives. When venturing out in the area of a new ministry, starting a new job or phase in our personal lives, or a new relationship we can become more vulnerable, especially if we've allowed God to slip into second or third place in our life.

Don't get down on yourself though, it is human nature to become engrossed or focused on these areas that are new or require more of our attention to excel in. Remember, though, to refocus on why those new areas of influence or intimacy are in your life- that is the plan of God for you to be a blessing- a person of authority who carries the Kingdom inside is paramount. So be prepared, because even Jesus himself was attacked when he was most vulnerable. Recall that after tempting Jesus Satan left him, but only "for a season".

I can go on an on, but the essential thing that you must know is that the strategy of the enemy is to suffocate your dream, the dream that God put on the inside of you.

Psalm chapter thirty-seven tells us that God will give us the desires of our heart. If you have a sincere desire and an authentic dream that lines up with the Word and is unique to you just as you are unique from everyone around you then you better believe that God has put that dream inside you. And if he put it inside you he didn't put it there so that it would go unfulfilled. NO, it is HIS desire that it would come to pass in *your* life.

God Wants You to Flourish

III John 2 "Beloved I wish above all things that thou would prosper and be in health even as your soul prospers"

A study of the word "prosper" in this passage shows

that it means journey or progress. And that is just what the Father wants for you… to progress in every area of your life. Not only does God want you to make progress in your spiritual walk, but he wants you to develop physically as you care for his temple (your body), and he especially wants you to develop in your soul realm; that is in the area of your mind, your will, and your emotions.

And *that* is the area where the enemy is most likely to strike. One thing you need to know, however, is that a snake in the natural will not swallow something that is bigger than the diameter at its widest part and even if it did it would literally kill him. Let me put that another way… Going back to our example of the garter snake, it is maybe an inch to an inch and a half at its widest section, that garter snake is not going after a possum that is eight to ten inches around. No way, he is going to stick to field mice, insects and small amphibians. Realize this brother and sister, the enemy knows he can't swallow you whole. Why? Well, for one reason "greater is He that is in you than he that is in the world" (I John 4:4)

But he will go after a part of you that can cause *you to take yourself out* if you are not vigilant.

You see, I know a lot of believers, many of whom are living the abundant life that God has in store for those who love him; but all too many are living their Christian lives as my Pastor would say as "weak worms in the dust". What I have found to be the cause of this in most cases is a time in their Christian walk where they believed God for something and it either seemingly did not come to fruition or they came against some opposition that knocked them off the track, and they NEVER got back on.

Paul gathered a pile of brushwood and, as he put it on the fire, a viper, driven out by the heat, fastened itself on his hand. Acts 28:3 (NIV)

Just because you labor in the house of God doesn't exempt you from the attacks of the enemy. Paul was in the midst of laboring in the new community he had landed on, helping to maintain the fire the natives had built to help stay warm in the rainy and cold weather, when the viper latched on to his hand. This was just *one* of the obstacles he faced throughout his ministry. So why should you be surprised when something comes your way to try to derail you.

Just because you don't see your dream happening now doesn't mean God has fallen off the throne, and opposition by no means indicates that you are out of the will of God. In fact I would be more concerned about whether or not I was in God's will if I didn't experience someone or some thing coming against me from time to time.

The Apostle of Opposition

If there is anything the life of the Apostle Paul reveals to us it is that opposition means you are precisely in the will of God. As a matter of fact when you withstand the opposition the enemy has planned for you it actually functions as a short cut to the things God has in store for you.

Relative Intensity

Since my mid teens I have been an avid fitness enthusiast. I've tried it all from running a marathon to lifting

28

weights. One thing I have gained from my experience in this type of training as well as in my education in the field of Chiropractic is an understanding for what it takes to change one's physique. While working for the Athletics Department at Morris Brown College in Atlanta, Ga. I was called upon to help their top athletes recover from injury and ideally stay injury free. I relied on the principle I am about to share with you in both instances. You see growth either in size, speed, strength, or muscular appearance is a product of something called *Relative Intensity*.

Let me give you an example. Suppose two friends decided to work out together, one of the friends has been training diligently for years and regularly lifts weights in excess of two hundred pounds. The other is scrawny, maybe one hundred pounds soaking wet and has never picked up anything heavier than a turkey drumstick. His idea of exercise is to fill up the tub, lift the stopper, and swim against the current. What would you expect if they embarked on a program in which they both lifted twenty pounds ten times each for arm curls? Do you think each would get the same results? After all they are lifting the same amount of weight and doing it the same amount of repetitions.

If you guessed the smaller of the two men would be most likely to increase his stamina, strength, and maybe even build some muscle you would be right. You may not have guessed the flip side of the equation though, and that is the bigger man, because he was not challenged with this form of workout, would actually "de-condition" because over the time of performing "relatively" less intense workouts he would lose strength, endurance, and size. When helping a football player recover from injury it was necessary for me to gauge where there effort needed to be to produce gains. Coming back from an injury would mean they were not as strong as what they were before their body was weakened. If I trained them too hard I risked a set back in their recovery. In a short season that could be disastrous for the team. By the same token if I did not challenge them enough they could show signs of recovery only to have their weakness exposed in competition. Picture this scenario, a new believer is taking on a challenge he has not prepared for, he hasn't spent much time in the word, he has the enthusiasm of a young convert but doesn't understand his position spiritually. Do you see how getting in over his head might cause him frustration and start him spiraling downward spiritually, emotionally, or even physically. Now imagine for a minute what would take place in the life of a believer who never had their faith challenged, who never had to face obstacles, or had their trust in God tested. It's no wonder so many Christians have become fat cats, and spiritually sluggish.

Behind Bars but Ahead of the Curve

Paul wrote over half of the New Testament mostly from behind prison cell bars. Ridiculed, imprisoned, spit on, cursed, reviled, beaten, and exiled are all terms that can be used to describe Paul's experiences. Did this mean he was out of God's will or that God wouldn't use him? No, just the opposite, it helped strengthen Paul and galvanize the Church. Now, relatively speaking, we may not need this level of resistance, but the resistance we do face is meant by the enemy to induce harm but used by God to increase us.

OPPOSITION DOESN'T MEAN YOU ARE
OUT OF GOD'S WILL. DID OPPOSITION
INDICATE DANIEL WAS OUT OF GOD'S WILL?
DID THE THREATENING VOICE OF GOLIATH
REPRESENT DAVID BEING OUT OF THE
DIVINE STRATEGY GOD HAD FOR HIS LIFE?
AND NO THE OPPOSITION YOU ARE
FACING DOESN'T MEAN YOU CAN'T OR
WON'T FULFILL GOD'S PLAN FOR YOU.

We are troubled on every side, yet not distressed; we are perplexed, but not in despair; Persecuted, but not forsaken; cast down, but not destroyed; Always bearing about in the body the dying of the Lord Jesus, that the life also of Jesus might be made manifest in our body (II Cor 4:8-10)

The Enemy's Best Efforts Are No Match for Us

Remember what the word says to us about such trials: "All things work together for good for those who love Him and are called according to his purpose" (Romans 8:28) Opposition doesn't mean you are out of God's will. Did opposition indicate Daniel was out of God's will? Did the threatening voice of Goliath represent David being out of the divine strategy God had for his life? And no the opposition you are facing doesn't mean you can't or won't fulfill God's plan for you. Like lifting weights in the gym challenges your muscles and causes them to grow, with each extra step beyond where you have gone against resistance before your faith and strength will grow, which is the will of God in Christ Jesus that we would go from faith to faith.

I can vividly recall one such example of this principle at work. In the mid to late 1990's the church we attended, and are still a part of today, Faith Fellowship Ministries World Outreach Center in New Jersey was bursting at the seams. The building we had in Edison, N.J. could no longer support our growing multicultural membership, which at the time was about seven thousand five hundred people and the leadership of the church began looking for a new piece of property. Under the direction of our Pastor, David T. Demola we found a property off of a major thoroughfare, the Garden State Parkway, and right on Main Street in Sayreville, N.J.. It was a prime location because of its visibility and proximity to several major roadways that could accommodate the regionality of a church that had members from North, Central, and Southern New Jersey, as well as Pennsylvania, and New York.

The only problem was that the political leaders in Sayreville didn't embrace the vision that we had for the property; in fact they were dead set against it. In an area that had not seen economic growth in years they steadfastly resisted our move to Sayreville, and at every town council meeting voted down our application, unanimously. You see these politicians had their sights set on getting big business in this location, but more to the point the snake, Satan, didn't want to see a faith filled church in this spiritually dead community, in an area known as a preacher's graveyard. With each passing denial the voices of so called men and women of faith began to whisper "This must not be God, if he wanted you on that land you wouldn't be going through such difficulty in obtaining it." "You need to find somewhere else to put your church, somewhere you are really wanted, since it is obvious you are not wanted there."

Thank God for a Pastor who believes the Word of God, "Let God be true and every man a liar." (Romans 3:4) Despite the opposition, even from close friends in the ministry, and under the direction of the Holy Spirit the Church continued to pursue our promised land until, we received a resounding victory when a judge ruled that Sayreville's town council, was unreasonable and unlawful in their opposition to our proposed purchase and vision for that land. God provided the victory because, through the leadership of Pastor Demola, Faith Fellowship was willing to shake off the snake in the area of opposition.

Resistance Builds Faith Muscles

Today, Faith Fellowship is thriving in it's "there" place; that is the place where God told us we *should* be. The church is right on Main Street and now has well over ten thousand members. Through the work of committed volunteers and the power of the Holy Spirit it is able to cater to a diverse population with services in English, Spanish, Portuguese, and Korean; not to mention an international school for ministers.

> GOD IS NO RESPECTER OF PERSONS,
> BUT, HE IS A RESPECTER OF FAITH.

The church, once scorned, is now a vital part of the rebirth and development of the area as new businesses and further development to the infrastructure in the form of new roadways and traffic patterns have followed. And what God can do for a church, HE will do for individuals as well. He is no respecter of persons, BUT, he is a respecter of faith. Strong, and more importantly growing faith is as powerful (if not more so) in me and you as it was in the Giants of faith recorded in the Bible.

You see what the enemy has meant for harm, despair and destruction in your life, what he has meant to crush your dreams, or cut off the oxygen of your progress is a tool in God's hand to build you up and strengthen you. Just as it takes the resistance of weight to build big physical muscles, with each bit of opposition and resistance you face and overcome the bigger your FAITH muscles become, and it will allow Him and you together to literally turn a minus into a plus for you.

Relative Resistance

The thing about resistance is that once you get used to overcoming it, at a certain level, the same level of resistance no longer fazes you, nor does it produce positive results. Going back to our example of weight lifting to build big muscles this is the primary reason most average body builders and people who regularly do low intensity exercise do not fully achieve their goals for improvement. It is the principal of relative resistance.

People who perform the same workout "routine" week after week, month after month, and year after year find they come up against a ceiling to their growth or fat loss goals. As a result many of them, and this is something I have witnessed over and over during my career, get bored or lose the drive to work out and give up. If the same people would periodically introduce a different type of exercise or challenge themselves more intensely on the same exercises they would find that they could literally explode through the ceiling.

Are you ready to explode through the ceiling? Have you finally gotten fed up with the status quo, of not seeing your life dramatically change after years of the same old same old? If your faith is going to grow then you are going to have to face and overcome challenges that you have never faced or conquered before. It's one thing to believe God to heal a headache, it's another to be faced with an "incurable disease" and have to trust God for a miracle. Its one thing to have the faith God can pay your $100 light bill, and another, altogether, to rely on Him to fund a worldwide ministry or business that supports one hundred full time employees.

Your faith is built on levels and you must be consistently increasing, otherwise you slide back. You've got to build it up one solid level at a time, with bricks that can hold the foundation.

What Ingredients are your Bricks made of?

I once saw a program on the History Channel that detailed the building of an ancient civilization that has since ceased to exist. The program talked about the fact that a part of one of their cities had been discovered, accidentally, underneath a present day city. From this discovery the archaeologist were able to determine the style of building and the layout of their once flourishing cities. The narrator of the program discussed the immaculate temples they built, and the drainage system they had developed that was visible in the remains of the once hidden structures of their society.

The entire find begged the question, however, of why did this civilization cease to exist? Was it because of enemy attacks or the result of an internal conflict. They pondered the idea of a natural disaster or a man made disaster such as a mass fire. Ultimately, though, the answer was found in the bricks on which the city was built. The experts analyzed the composition of the bricks in the structures that had been preserved under the existing city and found the fatal flaw in their construction.

As it turns out the city had been essentially built on MUD.

That's right, a close inspection of the bricks showed compelling evidence to convince the archaeologist assigned to the find that the large edifices, were put together by what amounted to mud and a very little straw. There was no evidence that they had been baked as brick to harden and solidify the structure such that when normal rains came they would gradually eat away at the structure weakening the foundation. It wasn't a big flood or storm that wrecked the city, but gradual wearing away at its infrastructure. Even more amazing was the revelation that the drainage system that was in place showed that they had knowledge of this flaw but didn't do anything about it, and so they were doomed by their refusal to act accordingly.

What are your bricks made out of? Have they been baked by the fire of God or has that passion waxed cold? Are you doing something right now about what you know to be wrong and needs to be corrected or are you just letting the chips fall where they may? It's never too late to see your situation turn around, and if you set your heart and fix your focus on God he can take your mess and turn it into a masterpiece.

SHAKE OFF THE SNAKE

The Pit was the Quickest Route to the Palace

Remember Joseph and his amazing coat. Remember Joseph and his dreams. You may recall Joseph dreamed big. He dreamed well beyond his position in life, he dreamed so big it infuriated the devil. That's right it infuriated the devil. You may be saying to yourself, I don't recall the devil being mentioned in the account of Joseph, it was his brothers that were angry with him, so angry in fact that they plotted to kill him.

And when they saw him afar off, even before he came near unto them, they conspired against him to slay him. And they said one to another, Behold, this dreamer cometh. Come now therefore, and let us slay him, and cast him into some pit, and we will say, Some evil beast hath devoured him: and we shall see what will become of his dreams. (Genesis 37:18-20)

I want to submit to you that it wasn't brotherly anger and jealousy that was the real enemy of Joseph, and in fact Joseph wasn't even the ultimate target. You see Joseph's purpose in the plan of God was essential to preserving the nation of Israel and ultimately the lineage of the savior of the world, the Lord Jesus Christ. So it was Satan who was really threatened by his dreams and visions of greatness and servant-hood. Joseph's brothers merely served as his vessels to carry out his strategy to thwart God's plan of salvation. And so they threw Joseph in the pit and planned on leaving him for dead.

A.J. RUBANO, D.C.

A Vested Interest

But God had a vested interest in Joseph, just as he has a vested interest in you. Because of that interest, that planned purpose He was not about to let Joseph be killed; and as a matter of fact took advantage of the situation to have Joseph moved into a position of influence, first in Potipher's house, and then, after a second attempt on Joseph's life, to Pharaoh's house, and position of second in command to Pharaoh himself.

I want you to see what Joseph realized at this stage in his life as he met with his brother's for the first time in so many years. Look at his perspective on the other side of the trial…

"What you meant for harm God meant for good"
Genesis 50:20

Even the enemy's most thought out, vicious attacks have nothing on you when you consider that God has a vested interest in who you are and whose you are.

> YES, SNAKES DO SWALLOW THEIR
> VICTIMS WHOLE AND ALIVE,
> BUT YOU ARE NOT A VICTIM,
> YOU ARE A VICTOR.

Yes, snakes do swallow their victims whole and alive, but you ARE NOT a victim, you are a VICTOR. The word of God doesn't just call you a winner it actually says you are MORE than a conqueror.

No, <u>in all these things</u> we are more than conquerors through him who loved us. Romans 8:28

Notice the words that precede you and I being more than conquerors. "In all these things.." refers to just about anything meant to side track your success in life. Isn't it good to know that for every conflict and problem God has the answer for you and it won't swallow you up. No it won't because you have this promise that you will come out on top.

Now that you know the enemy can't swallow you whole get back on course and watch God do wondrous things through you and in you.

Your Dreams: a Nightmare for Your Adversary

Get back to dreaming and when you do don't dream small dreams. Dream dreams that are worthy of the God of the universe. Shrinking back from great things doesn't serve you and it doesn't serve God. I know the religious mindset tells you to be satisfied with what you have, that you are lucky to have something at all; but God never says that. Why else would he be referred to as El Shaddai, the God that is "more than enough."

Believe it or not your dreams are tied directly to the kingdom of God being manifested here on earth. Like Joseph they were given to you for kingdom business. Oh sure, they may relate to a product or service your own business supplies and can meet the needs of the people in your community but they are given to you to further God's plan here on earth. That's why he wants you to have an enlarged vision of what the future holds.

Your dreams are meant to steer you away from evil as they did for the wise men after their pilgrimage to see the Christ child and were warned "in a dream" to take a different route home away from Herod the King (Matthew 2:12). Your dreams are meant to help you build and restore a heritage for God's people as they did with Nehemiah and helped sustain his men as they began the project to rebuild the wall around Jerusalem (Nehemiah). Your dreams are meant to help you overcome treachery as they did for Jacob in his dealings with his father in law, Laban (Genesis 31:11.) Your dreams are meant to enhance who you are and spur you on to excellence as dreams did for Daniel (Daniel 2:6), who while under the authority of an enemy people still advanced to prominence and a position of influence among the heathen of his day.

I am a doctor yes, but I am really in the dreams business. When people come to see me they are not asking me to just take their pain away. What they are really seeking is the ability to play golf or tennis a few times per week again. Some want to be able to travel to far off lands on legs that can carry them up the steps of a Great Wall, or around the roads that lead to Rome. Others are envisioning being able to pick up their grandchildren and enjoy their retirement years as actively as they did their pre-retirement days. They come to me to help them fulfill their plans for the future.

If I am to do that I must prove to them that I am the one who can help and that they have within them the ability to heal; more so than that I must provide the motivation in tangible form and the path to get to their destination. That is why I give them a written description of both the problem at hand and the solution to overcome that difficulty.

I find, more than anything else, it is this path that helps

SHAKE OFF THE SNAKE

get results. When the gains are slow, as long as my practice members recognize they are on the path we have agreed upon they will find a way to overcome the obstacles that stand in the way. They will wake up early if they have to, they will do a few extra sets of painful repetitions if need be, and they will follow my recommendations for home care.

Your dreams, while a target of the enemy, are given to you by God as a source of energy to you (Habbakuk 2:2) and to cause you to withstand and prevail against the attacks of the snake. If you write them down and keep them before you always they will embolden you to accomplish the very things you were born to do, build the kingdom and bruise the head of the forces that stand against it.

"THE INTENTION OF EVERY ATTACK
OF THE ENEMY IN YOUR LIFE IS TO
CREATE IMBALANCES THAT KEEP YOU
FROM PURSUING THE PROMISES GOD
HAS FOR YOU AND YOUR EFFECTIVENESS
IN SHARING THE GOSPEL OF JESUS
CHRIST WITH A DYING WORLD."

"EVEN IF A SNAKE IS NOT POISONOUS,
IT SHOULD PRETEND TO BE VENOMOUS."

CHANAKYA

CHAPTER 4

POISON CONTROL

"Resentment is like drinking poison and then hoping it will kill your enemies."

Nelson Mandela

We've all seen movies or heard stories about campers or hikers out in the forest who come across a rattle snake and are bitten. Of course in these cases the story line almost always shifts to a race against time and last minute, last gasp heroics. This kind of heroism often reminds me of the way God has worked in my life through the years, he is never late, and usually not early, but he is always right on time when it comes to meeting the needs and delivering his children. I love the fact that He is willing to heroically save us from all the enemies' plans, but I want to talk with you for just a moment about the process of poisoning that may require such saving from.

Different types of snakes poison their prey in different ways. Some release toxins that damage muscle tissue, others unleash substances that interfere with the ability of blood to clot, while others have venom that may cause the blood to clot too much.

When it comes to snakes, especially here in the United States, most of us think about the deadly rattle snake. From its fierce eyes to its rattling tail the rattle snake inspires a physical reaction from nearly anyone you speak with. The Mojave rattler is one such snake with extremely deadly venom. The venom of this snake, found throughout Arizona, contains a substance known as a neurotoxin.

Direct Disconnect

Before we get into just how a snake poison works we need to understand this basic information about the body's nervous system. Our nerve system has nerve cells called NEURONS. A neuron can be thought of as a telephone receiver. Neurons in our bodies are connected by a Neurotransmitter (a chemical messenger), which for all intents and purposes can be considered to be your telephone wire or fiber optic line. Using these neurotransmitters and neurons the brain is able to stay in constant and accurate communication with all of the other body parts and systems.

Now, according to experts in the field of snake study, neurotoxins are a protein in snake venom that is among the most deadly. The proteins in the venom get into the blood stream and begin to break down the normal communication that is supposed to take place from one neuron to another by interfering with the neurotransmitter. The result is that either no message or a jumbled message is delivered, if not treated quickly this will lead to paralysis or even death.

Communication with God is Your Life Link

Now the enemy understands that our communication

with God is the vital link to our living for God and fulfilling the plan and purpose God has for us. The last thing he wants is to see a believer grow in grace and faith through accurate communication with the Father. The venom of the enemy while not an actual "neurotoxin" may as well be for it is geared to cut off totally or jumble your connection to Daddy God. The poison that he injects into the system of a believer is meant to hinder your prayer life and take your focus off of your need for your connection to Jesus. Although there are many different types of snake toxins there really is only one intent and that is to create some type of imbalance that is strong enough to disable the effectiveness of its prey.

The intention of every attack of the enemy in your life is to create imbalances in your life that keep you from pursuing the promises God has for you and your effectiveness in sharing the gospel of Jesus Christ with a dying world.

The Poison of Pride

Pride goeth before destruction, and an haughty spirit before a fall. (Proverbs 16:18)

Pride is a deceptive and subtle vehicle that the enemy will use to infect the thought process of God's people. It was the poison of pride that led to Satan, the former top angel and minister of music in heaven, being booted out of heaven with a host of other rebellious (un)heavenly beings

He replied " I saw Satan fall like lightning from heaven." (Luke 10:18)

It was almost as if thoughts of grandeur and delusions

45

of his own greatness seeped into his mind and over-rode the instructions that he knew to be true, so much so that he seemingly had no control over his own actions.

If you're not careful you can be tricked into thinking you don't need God, that you can handle your situation on your own. If you have teenage children, or perhaps were one at one time you may know all too well how the teenage mind is programmed to this type of thinking. I can't tell you how many times, as a teenager, I responded to my parents' advice or warnings about a variety of topics by saying "I know", while rolling my eyes behind their backs (now, many teens will do it right in front of their parents' faces); only to find out after suffering the consequences of my actions that they were right all along. The problem was I had a preconceived notion or thought in my head, and I didn't see the need to move off that thought, especially since I had reconciled in my mind that it would bring great satisfaction to my flesh.

The wicked, through the pride of his countenance, will not seek after God: God is not in all his thoughts (Psalm 10:4)

Pride, if we are not careful, can be like a drug that once it's in our system causes us to crave it more and more. The more you get, the more you need. It has led to the fall of not only men, but of nations and empires. The power and intoxicating effect of pride were such that the devil tried his best to poison Jesus with it.

And the devil, taking him up into an high mountain, shewed unto him all the kingdoms of the world in a moment of time. And the devil said unto him, All this power will I give thee, and the glory of them: for that is

delivered unto me; and to whomsoever I will I give it. If thou therefore wilt worship me, all shall be thine. (Luke 4:5-7)

The Word- Your Best Defense against Satan's Lies

Had Jesus accepted Satan's offer he would have had the world at his feet, utter power in every worldly sense of the word. How easy it would have been for him to get caught up in the euphoria of this offer of limitless earthly power and authority. At least that is what Satan wanted him to believe. Don't fool yourself and think this was not a *real* temptation for Jesus. It was. In fact I believe that when the scripture says "he was in all points tempted" just as we are, this very incident was at the top of the list. Thank God for the second part of that verse "yet without sin", otherwise God's Plan A would have been thwarted.

For many of us it is no different. We like power, we like to be in control, and we want the last say on a matter. If you had to suffer under a strong or heavy handed parent, teacher, or boss you relish the chance to assert yourself forcefully. You want to "break out" and display your talents and skills. As is human nature when we get a little, we soak up more.

The Devil Wants to Take You Down, But God Will Do All to Help You Up

God is well aware of the human condition though. He is not ignorant of our weaknesses. In fact He saw the devil himself go through his own ego trip, full of pride, heaven's minister of music as it were. He became self absorbed , self infatuated, and lost sight of where the source of his brilliance had come from. In the very face of God he demanded his due, and led the mutiny of other angels deceived by his own bravado only to be bolted right out of heaven.

It's no wonder, he'd like nothing more than to see you follow his footsteps; falling for yourself and by yourself. Yes by yourself, even though he would have you think that "everyone" is doing it. But, Glory to God, that is not the Father's direction for you, it's not His plan. Instead of waiting for the poison to knock out our communication senses he provides the antidote. He reminds us not "to think more highly of ourselves than we ought." (Romans 12:3) He revealed in the very human aspect of Jesus of Nazareth's resistance of all that the devil offered him that we too can resist Satan's offerings. He tells us that we are the very apple of his eye, reminding us that we are fearfully and wonderfully made (Psalm 17:8 and 139:14). In other words he created us with greatness of thought.

For many, pride is merely a defense mechanism against their own preconceived shortcomings. They say within themselves I can't let the outside world see me for the nothing that I *think* I am or else they'll hate me like I hate myself. Strong words, yet too often true. So what do they do, they hide behind their mask of pride. I can't tell you how many times the people who have attempted to be the most hurtful and most resistant to God in my life were people who felt the sting of feeling like they were nothing on the inside, so much so that it was all they could do to soften the sting by building up this rough, prideful exterior. Unfortunately the prideful attitude that was supposed to protect them was a mere sham, and was no protection at all.

SHAKE OFF THE SNAKE

See Yourself As God Sees You

Brother and Sister you overcome the poison of pride by shaking off the snake and applying the balm, the antidote. You shake off the snake in this area by reminding yourself that God is the author of all things good, and you need to stay connected to him. Jesus didn't go to the cross because there were only a select few who needed the benefit of a savior; NO, he did it because we all fall short of the glory of GOD in our day to day lives. You overcome the poison of pride by daily talking with God in private in your prayer closet, AND allowing Him to speak into your life both through the Word and what He imparts to you.

Now before you think Christianity is a call to self debasement or self humiliation recall that God reminds us to look in the mirror, and not to see ourselves as poor, weak, or defenseless BUT also not independent of him. He tells us not to think "more" highly of ourselves (Romans 12:3) which carries with it the connotation that we may still think of ourselves in high regard. He saves us from the colossal fall from grace that was reserved for the devil and his cohorts and softens the sting of our short fall from self aggrandizement by making it O.K. to still think we are something. And yes we are, because if we look further into that mirror we will recognize that we are made in the very image and likeness of God. (Genesis 1: 26) In fact, in the area of dominion and authority here on Earth we are positionally to stand in the stead of God. We are his "under shepherds" and we are supposed to think, speak, and act as Jesus did when he was here. He didn't see it as robbery when he walked the Earth as a man to be equal with God (Philippians 2:6). Now I am not saying we are God or equal in power or authority to the Almighty, what I am saying is the authority we have been granted, standing in his stead comes with the full weight of all heaven has to offer. It's just like when a police officer stands in the center of an intersection or flashes his badge and says "Stop, in the name of the law" people have to respect that or suffer the consequences, not because of who that officer is as an individual, but because of the government he represents.

That being said, it is sad that so many of God's people walk around without really understanding who they are and so, they cover up and put on the false face of pride. It (pride) is a cheap imitation when compared to the real royalty we have always been destined to represent.

The Poison of Jealousy and Competition

Then came to him the mother of Zebedees children with her sons, worshipping him, and desiring a certain thing of him. And he said unto her, What wilt thou? She saith unto him, Grant that these my two sons may sit, the one on thy right hand, and the other on the left, in thy kingdom. But Jesus answered and said, Ye know not what ye ask. Are ye able to drink of the cup that I shall drink of, and to be baptized with the baptism that I am baptized with? They say unto him, We are able. And he saith unto them, Ye shall drink indeed of my cup, and be baptized with the baptism that I am baptized with: but to sit on my right hand, and on my left, is not mine to give, but it shall be given to them for whom it is prepared of my Father. And when the ten heard it, they were moved with indignation against the two brethren. Matthew 20: 20-24

Another ploy of the enemy, one very closely linked to the poison of pride is the poison of jealousy and competition. The devil's hope is that in swallowing this that it will knock out not only individual Christians, but serve to be the force that severs the ties that bind the Church together in unity.

When a neuro-toxic snake poison hits the nervous system it can have the effect of cutting off communication not only from the brain to certain body systems but also *between* systems, causing major shifts in chemical balance that literally turn one body system against another as they fight for survival.

What happens when you and I start focusing on what we don't have in relationship to what others do have? Whether it be STUFF, or position we get into strife and contention mostly because we fear we are going to be on the outside looking in. Our defense mechanisms kick in, we get into the mind set of survival, and we go into what I like to call PROTECT MODE. So, like the world we fall all over each other stepping on one another trying to be the pastor's favorite, or maneuver so we can be in the place and position of authority or power in our church or department. The needs of the other no longer matter because I've "got to get mine".

How Do You Want Your Reward?

Let me put this to you in a way that might be more familiar. A couple my wife and I were once close with had been married for a few years when things in their relationship began to go haywire. The husband had been called in on a special project at work and as a result saw his hours nearly double. As he became more engrossed in his assignment he neglected his young wife and she grew distant and jealous. She began to think in her heart that he was not working but instead having an affair. She decided, as the saying goes, "What's good for the goose is good for the gander" and began an illicit affair with one of her co-workers. Within a few months this once happy couple was in the throes of a divorce, all because each one of them became caught up in their part and lost sight of the needs of the other. In the end both scored pyrrhic victories- as he got a promotion, and she her revenge- but what a sad price to pay.

Jesus had a saying for situations such as this, "you have your reward". In other words, the reward you get at that present time is all the reward you get when you take that approach. God has not called us to a life of surviving, or just getting by but to a life of thriving. Jesus advised that we ought to seek our approval in secret from our heavenly father, who would, at the proper time reward us openly and I can tell you with certainty that His idea of reward is exceedingly and abundantly above all you could ever hope or imagine. Remember to shake off the snake in the area of jealousy and competition because your promotion doesn't come from man but from God himself. When others wrong you as sometimes will be the case allow God to be God. Though the wicked will prevail for a time they will soon be cut off and your dreams will come to fruition (Psalm 37).

The Right Way to Handle Competition

But Jesus called them unto him, and said, Ye know that the princes of the Gentiles exercise dominion over them, and they that are great exercise authority upon them. But it shall not be so among you: but whosoever will be great among you, let him be your minister; And whosoever will be chief among you, let him be your ser-

vant: (Matt 20:25-27)

Jesus and the disciples did just that, putting an end to contention before it even began. When you try to outdo each other in service, it becomes rather difficult to come into strife. Just the opposite occurs, unity and looking out for the needs of others becomes the antidote.

> WHEN YOU TRY TO OUTDO EACH OTHER IN SERVICE, IT BECOMES RATHER DIFFICULT TO COME INTO STRIFE.

If you are going to shake off the snake and not be harmed by the poison of jealousy and competition you are going to have to keep communicating with your Christian brothers and sisters, and by that I don't mean just the ones that go to your church. Realize that competition between churches ultimately weakens our witness with the unbelieving world who needs to see the right way to handle the need for recognition. We are going to have to focus on putting the needs of others even above our own and trust God that he won't leave us out. Instead of gossiping or speaking ill against our brother and sister we are going to have to learn to obey the word and pray for them, pray with them, and speak well of them. Remember that when it comes to recognition in God, the way up is the way down; in other words your greatness doesn't come from how many people who serve you, but the amount and attitude in which you serve others.

A.J. RUBANO, D.C.

The Poison of Greed

For the love of money is the root of all evil: which while some coveted after, they have erred from the faith, and pierced themselves through with many sorrows. I Timothy 6:10

In the early 1500's the Spaniard, Francisco Pizarro conquered Peru and with it brought an influx of Gold and tales of riches to Spain. One such tale that became prominent was that of El Dorado, an Indian Chief who once yearly sprinkled Gold Dust all over his body before plunging into a nearby lake. The tale grew to the point to where the people believed the city of El Dorado literally had streets paved with gold.

It was not long before Gonzalo Pizarro, Francisco's brother, led an expedition in search of this golden city taking with him hundreds of explorers and thousands of slaves and animals. As he ventured into the jungles of Peru he killed anyone who he deemed was withholding information concerning the whereabouts of El Dorado, the great golden city. As word spread about his terror the natives knew the only way to save themselves was to come up with stories to keep Pizarro on his quest, and so they led him further and further into the jungle with more tales of palatial riches. With his expedition team either dying off or deserting, Pizarro eventually called off the expedition and came back to Spain not only empty handed, but a mere shadow of his former self. And so it was for all that followed him in search of El Dorado, a hunger for its riches leading to a steady downfall in Spain. With greed came neglect and with neglect came financial ruin and poverty of the soul and spirit.

Are You In Search of the Blessing or the Blesser?

So it is with the poison of greed. Greed separates us from God, causing us to neglect our relationship with the Almighty. When we seek the blessings more than the blesser we enable the things we seek to function as idols in our lives. That may sound harsh, and you are probably saying within yourself I am not an idol worshipper. But the truth is if you put the love of THINGS before God you are just that.

Don't get me wrong here, I am a firm believer that God wants to see All of His children blessed and prosperous, but there is a big difference between prospering God's way and the world's way. The Apostle Paul called it trusting in "uncertain riches", Jesus referred to it as "mammon". But it all comes back to focusing on the wrong thing, Things.

If it's important to God It Should be Important to Me

I recall a story recounted by Rev. Jesse Duplantis in which he shared about his enjoyment for motorcycle riding. He shared how the Lord had blessed him with this magnificent bike, and how it was more than he would have or could have purchased on his own. I can picture him right now, on that Harley Davidson cruising down the road, wind in his face, smiling and riding with Jesus. He went on to say he asked God why he would do something like that for him, and in a way only Rev. Duplantis can put it he said the Lord replied, "Because I love you Jesse, and I know it's important to you." Anyway, on one particular occasion he was riding that Harley and he came to a rest area where he picked up some food, I think it was a chili dog, but don't quote me on that. As he was eating his lunch he saw another biker sitting at one of the tables, and on an urging by the Holy Spirit he walked up to the man, a complete stranger, found out what he wanted to eat and brought it back to him, got to know him a little better and then he shared the good news about Jesus.

It was a small amount of time and money to Jesse Duplantis, but it was significant to the man. He gave his heart to Jesus that day. As he resumed his ride Jesse heard the voice of the Lord say to him, "Jesse, what did you do that for?" to which he replied "Because I love you Lord, and I know *that* was important to you."

You see God doesn't see anything wrong with you having STUFF. He even says as much in his word.

But seek ye first the kingdom of God, and his righteousness; and all these things shall be added unto you. (Matthew 6:33)

No, your Heavenly Father does not have a problem with you having things so long as those things don't have you. When it comes to the things that are high on God's list of priorities at the very top of the list is people. He doesn't want one person to perish, He wants everyone to choose life in Jesus Christ and He will go to great lengths to help people make the right choices.

Recognizing What Belongs To God

In this day and age all too often we see people abused at the expense of money. Businesses, organizations, and even ministries see people as disposable items, like the hand towels in their wash rooms. Under the guise of self preservation corporations lay off thousands of workers, many of

SHAKE OFF THE SNAKE

whom may have been responsible for the success of the company to begin with. Thankfully God doesn't work this way......and he doesn't want you and me to either.

If we follow the instruction God has laid out for us in the area of finances we will see that we can shake off the snake in the area of greed AND walk in supernatural abundance; because, despite what you may have been taught the two are not mutually exclusive, but linked together.

Rich Man, Poor Man

In Luke 12:16-20 Jesus tells of the exploits of a "certain rich man". Although he doesn't go into great detail about how the man obtained his wealth it doesn't appear on the surface that he did anything dishonest, unethical, or illegal to become rich, and yet Jesus referred to him as a fool.

How could a hard working, honest entrepreneur who saves his money be considered a fool? By today's standards we would say he is a shrewd businessman and call him a success, not a fool. But Jesus calls him a fool. Let's see why....

And he spake a parable unto them, saying, The ground of a certain rich man brought forth plentifully: And he thought within himself, saying, What shall I do, because I have no room where to bestow my fruits? And he said, This will I do: I will pull down my barns, and build greater; and there will I bestow all my fruits and my goods. And I will say to my soul, Soul, thou hast much goods laid up for many years; take thine ease, eat, drink, and be merry. But God said unto him, Thou fool, this night thy soul shall be required of thee: then whose shall those things be,

which thou hast provided? (Luke 12: 16-20)

Once you read what this rich man thought about what he had and you have an understanding of what is important to God it's easy to understand why Jesus called him a fool. First this man had no concept of the other people who were responsible for helping him accumulate his wealth. There is no mention of those that plowed the fields or harvested the crops, or even of those that took his product to market, or kept his books.

How often have we fallen into this same trap. I mean, especially in this day and age of automation, do we even stop to consider what it takes to have all of our needs met. Think about the clothes you have on, it's very likely you have shoes from one country, undergarments produced by another, and a suit from somewhere else. We have never been as interdependent on the world as a whole's resources as we are today; and yet, perhaps, have never to this degree taken these blessings for granted.

But, not only did this rich man fail to recognize his dependence, or at the very least his need for the assistance from humanity, he also failed to realize that God is his source for everything in this life. Within the thought process of this man, everything relied on, depended upon, and came back to I. He said, "What shall *I* do"; "*I* have no room where to bestow *my* fruits". He continued by saying "This will *I* do"...... "*I* will say to *my* soul.. take *thine* ease...." There was no acknowledgement of thanks to God or the role he could play in helping someone else, not even a family member or close friend.

I would say it is more than probable he didn't have any really close friends, because he used and disrespected the ones he had. If he was married or had children, in all likelyhood he failed to give them the attention and love they needed to thrive and meet their potential. He was greedy for money, but not just money, but also for acknowledgement and credit; the greed wasn't reserved for one area, but pervaded his whole life. He was a fool because he couldn't render to people and to God what rightfully belonged to them.

Give God His Due

There are certain things that belong to God, and I am not just talking the financial things. Starting with the Tree of the Knowledge of Good and Evil in the Garden of Eden there are things that are meant to be set apart to God and left to his plans and purposes.

> WHETHER IT'S YOUR TITHE, FINANCIAL OFFERINGS, FAMILY, BUSINESS, TIME, OR YOUR TALENT GOD IS CALLING YOU TO RECOGNIZE WHAT IT IS THAT BELONGS TO AND NEEDS TO BE DEDICATED TO HIM.

And when we fail to recognize those things, we are separated from his presence, just as Adam and Eve were separated from Him and evicted from the Garden. (Genesis 3)

Whether it's your tithe, financial offerings, family, business, time, or your talent God is calling you to recognize what it is that belongs to and needs to be dedicated to Him. Shake off the snake by resisting the lies of the enemy regarding the things that are Holy unto the Lord. Render unto God what is due him, give to Him the glory and honor He is due, give back to Him the tithe and the offering and you will have more than enough, your needs and desires will be met and He won't make it a painful or sorrowful thing.

The Poison of Religion

Of all the attitudes, thought processes, and mind sets that potentially function as poisons in our lives there is perhaps none more deadly than religion. My friend, Bishop Raymond Moss, called this way of thinking "Religiosity."

It is a set of ideas not based on what God details in *His* book, but rather on the traditions of men. Religious thinkers don't care as much about *being* right as they do about *looking* right. Rather than fearing God and trembling at His word their every action hinges on the perception of men.

Sadly this type of poison is a subtle killer dulling the senses and lulling the victim into a false sense of his own security. Instead of bringing the person closer to God, the practice of powerless religious exercises only serves to widen the gulf. Rote prayers and a steady stream of good works, by themselves, without a heart connection to Jesus won't help you to know God any more than a few words of shallow conversation and gold trinkets will bring true closeness between a husband and wife. Husbands don't get intimate with their wives by following a series of preconceived rituals or memorized movements. They draw near by knowing their wives emotionally and communicating with them at the deepest of levels. A man who thinks he is emotionally bonded to his wife because she sacrifices her body for him before drifting off to unfulfilled sleep can easily find himself on the outside looking in before he knows what hit him. The same is true for anyone who thinks he can buy oneness with God through personal or financial sacrifice without finding out what is important to the creator of the universe. We were created for the express purpose of worship. The bible tells us as much when it reveals that God is looking for those who will worship Him in spirit and in truth (John 4: 23). Anything less is a mere sham, an exercise in futility.

Relationship, not rituals, is what the Father was after when he sacrificed his only begotten Son on the cross. How tragic that anyone would substitute a shallow means of self justification for the real intimacy that is available to those who really hunger for God's presence in their lives.

Hallucinogenic Effects

In addition to its lulling properties the poison of religion acts like a hallucinogen, paradoxically, blinding the recipient to his or her own faults while simultaneously improving the ability to see shortcomings in others. It turns the eye of judgment meant to bring us to the one who forgives off ourselves and on to those who we should be directing to the healer. Jesus never condemned sinners by pointing out their iniquities; instead he directed them toward their God ordained destiny. He didn't focus on the sin; he helped them look heavenward by causing them to see the path to their potential without the heaviness of guilt, shame, and poor self image weighing them down. Contrast that with the approach of the religious elite who at every opportunity would use the mistakes of those out in the world to bolster their claim of superiority. What we should be doing is asking ourselves "what in the world does something that someone else does or doesn't do have to do with my personal walk with God?" We should be working out our own salvation with fear and trembling before the Lord, instead we get caught up in finger pointing and comparing ourselves to other temporal beings instead of the eternal and immortal king.

A case in point is the account commonly referred to as "the woman caught in the act of adultery." A group of Pharisees brought this woman to Jesus to show just how righteous they were and to see if they could cast doubt on Jesus' character.

And the scribes and Pharisees brought unto him a woman taken in adultery; and when they had set her in the midst, They say unto him, Master, this woman was taken in adultery, in the very act. Now Moses in the law commanded us, that such should be stoned: but what sayest thou? John 8: 3-5

They condemned the woman to death by stoning for her indecent act. My first question is what of the man with whom she slept? And how did they catch her in the act to begin with?

Instead of falling prey to their trap Jesus perceived their religious hearts and turned the tide quickly with a declaration of his own.

This they said, tempting him, that they might have to accuse him. But Jesus stooped down, and with his finger wrote on the ground, as though he heard them not. So when they continued asking him, he lifted up himself, and said unto them, He that is without sin among you, let him first cast a stone at her. And again he stooped down, and wrote on the ground. And they

SHAKE OFF THE SNAKE

which heard it, being convicted by their own conscience, went out one by one, beginning at the eldest, even unto the last: and Jesus was left alone, and the woman standing in the midst. When Jesus had lifted up himself, and saw none but the woman, he said unto her, Woman, where are those thine accusers? hath no man condemned thee? She said, No man, Lord. And Jesus said unto her, Neither do I condemn thee: go, and sin no more. John 8:6-11

The Lord knew that true spirituality arises from restoration, not condemnation (Galatians 6:1). He was sinless and could have easily hurled a stone at this adulteress. He chose not to, preferring to use the liberty at his disposal to convey life to this child of God.

One Finger Pointing Away,
Four Pointing Right Back at You

Jesus had harsh words for the religious crowd. In this account in John some have surmised, and I tend to agree that, he may have written the various concealed indiscretions of the religious accusers causing them to slip away as the shame of their own wrong doing pierced through their hearts. It's true that we should be careful when pointing the accusing finger at someone because there are four others that are pointing in the opposite direction and aimed right back at me.

Matthew chapter twenty-three records a monologue aimed at the religious leaders of Jesus' day in which he chastised them for making hoops for people to jump through to get into heaven and for excusing themselves for "omitting the weightier practices of the law" (v. 23). Jesus called these religious folk clean on the outside yet filthy internally, fools, blind guides, pretentious, hypocritical, full of iniquity, and killers of the prophets. And then he asks a question.

Ye serpents, ye generation of vipers, how can ye escape the damnation of hell? Matthew 23: 33

He referenced them as aggressive and deadly snakes. He was well aware the harm that religion generates. He witnessed the way church leadership trained the young and hungry souls right out of salvation as blind guides leading the blind (Matthew 23:15). He saw first hand how powerful the poison of a little religious thinking could turn into a pervasive mind set spreading from one victim to the next (Galatians 5:9). Jesus said that the day will come when there will be those who will stand before the throne of God, awaiting the prize of a submitted life, and tell of all their accomplishments done in his name only to hear in response "I never knew you, depart from me you workers of iniquity." (Matthew 7: 23).

That is why religion is the most toxic of all poisons. For a religious mind damnation to hell is *almost* inescapable, *almost*. Jesus asked the question knowing that the hearts of many he spoke to would not turn and still it broke his heart; for like a hen wants to protect her chicks Jesus wanted to gather all Israel to himself. In his final words to the religious leaders he attempted to show them the cure for what ailed them, and yet again they missed it dismissing it as the ramblings of an infidel.

For I say unto you, Ye shall not see me henceforth, till ye shall say, Blessed is he that cometh in the name of the Lord. Matthew 23: 39

SHAKE OFF THE SNAKE

Just because that religious crowd missed it, doesn't mean you have to. While Jesus' words ring of a prophetic declaration for the fate of those relying on their own goodness, or awaiting a political messiah they also pronounce the way to God; these powerful words "ye shall not see me....till ye shall say...." reveal that heaven and all its blessings are in your mouth. The way to shake off the snake and rid your self of that religious poison is to simply let the words from your mouth "bless the Lord" and recognize that no matter how good you think you are or what rewards your deeds have garnered for you they all pale in comparison to what the Son has done on your behalf. They are wood, hay, and stubble to the silver, gold and precious stones that are found in a relationship with Jesus (I Corinthians 3:12)

Believers Have Poison Protection

Whether it be religious thinking, greed, jealousy, pride, lust, or any other poisonous weapon the enemy has in store for you there is one sure fire protection reserved for ALL believers. It is the name of Jesus. Scripture tells us that Jesus is the name that has been given above every other name, that at the name of Jesus every knee shall bow and every tongue confess that He is Lord. (Phil 2:9-10) Greed? That's a name! Pride? That's a name too! So are POVERTY, and JEALOUSY, CANCER, and DEPRESSION. These are all names that are under our feet as believers in the name of JESUS. The name of JESUS gives us authority over the enemy.

And these signs will accompany those who believe: In my name they will drive out demons; they will speak

A.J. RUBANO, D.C.

in new tongues; **they will pick up snakes with their hands; and when they drink deadly poison, it will not hurt them at all;** they will place their hands on sick people, and they will get well." Mark 16:17-18

Jesus gives you the assurance of poison protection. When you pick up a snake it will not hurt you, *unless you let it.* Now, before you think I've gone off the deep end, please realize that HE is not saying you should go into the forest and grab a rattlesnake by the tail and confess it can't hurt me. Indeed three out of every seven snake bites reported are classified as "illegitimate", meaning they occurred while the snake was either being mishandled or molested by the victim. Purposely toying with a rattlesnake is just the spirit of DUMB. What the word is saying is that when you come across an obstacle or a seemingly dangerous situation in your life He has a way of escape for you. He is saying that in this world tough times are going to come your way, attacks on your physical body, attacks on your emotional and spiritual well being, and yes, attacks on your finances. But based on your belief in him AND your willingness to follow his prescription to you and be obedient to His written and spoken word He will cause you and enable you to function in a supernatural anointing that will not only protect you from the destructive thoughts of your adversary, BUT, also allow you to be a vessel to bring that same strength, healing, and deliverance to others.

Overcoming Self Inflicted Wounds

While it is easy to accuse the enemy of poisoning the hearts and minds of the unsuspecting and leaving them for dead the truth of the matter is none of us escapes culpability when it comes to undermining the virtuous lives God

66

wants for everyone. It is undeniable that the snake corrupts us with the whispers and precisely placed flattery that lead to greedy, prideful, and jealous impulses; but by the same token we are just as guilty for the thoughts we give credence to which enhance the effect of the poison in our life. As you confess the name of Jesus over the "titles" that have been adversarial remember to "cast down imaginations" whether they be delusions of grandeur or vile fantasies at work within you; and "bring into captivity" all of your thoughts." (II Corinthians 10:5)

As you resist the devil, that crafty snake, understanding your level of accountability will help you become more adept at disarming the enemy. You see, as long as you believe that you have no control and that he is the one pulling the strings you will feel and be powerless against his devices; but once you see that you do have a measure of control the God that is within you is able to rise up and help you overcome even the most deadly poison. That is why we are urged to recall that the weapons of our warfare are not carnal, but mighty through God to the pulling down of strongholds. (II Corinthians 10:4). With the lass (a cutlass, referred to as a lass in West Indian culture, is a sharp machete used to chop down sugar cane) that is our tongue and the word of God on our lips we can pull down the strongholds and cut the poisonous snake into bits and pieces.

"IF YOU FIND YOURSELF GOING
THROUGH THE MOTIONS, CONSUMED
WITH THOUGHTS OF WORK AND WORRIES
INSTEAD OF WORSHIP; OR IF YOU ARE AL-
WAYS PLANNING YET NEVER PRAYING YOU
ARE PROBABLY HAVING A THORNY
GROUND EXPERIENCE."

"THE WORLD OF MEN IS DREAMING,
IT HAS GONE MAD IN ITS SLEEP,
AND A SNAKE IS STRANGLING IT,
BUT IT CAN'T WAKE UP."

DH LAWRENCE

CHAPTER 5

ALL CHOKED UP

"When we long for life without difficulties,
remind us that oaks grow strong in contrary winds
and diamonds are made under pressure"

Peter Marshall

As a child and even into young adulthood I had a persistent dream. Actually it was more of a nightmare, because it seemed <u>*so real*</u>, and literally took my breath away. The dream was very real to me because it involved and vividly portrayed in my mind recollections of the area where I was born and raised. In the small town of Lakewood, N.J. right at the corner of the two main roadways that passed through the center of our town, there was a small sized lake. This lake, which was visible from the church I attended was named Lake CaroSalJo, so named for three sisters, Carol, Sallie, and Josephine, who had drown there in either the 1950's or 60's. I had heard the story from my parents and others so many times that I felt like I had been there when the boat they were in capsized and they were unable to swim to the shoreline some three hundred yards away. I could picture them trying to swim to the surface, hands waving trying to push up to the top only to fall right back to the bottom because they lacked the stamina to push just a few more strokes.

To get to the point, in this dream that I had over and over, *I* was the one falling off of a dock that crossed over the lake, frantically wading to get to the top to reach the surface of the lake. As real as anything I ever felt was the inability to gasp to take a breath of fresh air, to fill my lungs with oxygen. I could feel myself being tugged down, scrunching my face in determination as I poured forth the effort to break free to the surface, doing anything possible to come to the top and live. The dream always ended the same, as I awoke, soaked in perspiration, and took a big gasp of air, thankful that it had only been a dream.

As real as that dream was, that frantic feeling of being sapped of the vital nutrient of oxygen to my brain and vital organs, there are believers today that are living and literally being deflated as they feel the crushing effects of the weighty issues in their life.

The snake kills by Process of Constriction

Still others, like seed sown among thorns, hear the word; but the worries of this life, the deceitfulness of wealth and the desires for other things come in and choke the word, making it unfruitful. Mark 4:18-19

Of the four different types of soil described by Jesus in this parable of the sower, none is more difficult to swallow the plight of than the one described as being thorny ground. Jesus went on to say that the type of person which is represented by this soil would actually hear and receive the blessing of the word of God, but then be moved off of this firm footing by deceit, desires, and the cares and worries of this world. (v 18-19)

This is the person who you look at and say, man they have so much potential, they could do so much in the kingdom of God. I am sure these are the souls that frustrate the pastors of many churches.

The tendency is to think of these as people who came in the church one day, heard a message that tickled their ears, said a quick prayer, and were born again, left excited to be a new believer, and were never seen again. But if we look closely at the passage we might find that probably isn't the type of person this refers to. No, what these verses describe is a process of constriction; a slow and steady death.

This would make it seem much more likely that the "thorny ground" group is not the people on the outside of the church living for the devil with no concern for what God has for them. The "thorny ground" group is more likely walking around the church, working, and in some cases leading in the church. If you find yourself going through the motions, consumed with thoughts of work and worries instead of worship; or if you are always planning yet never praying this is probably you.

The problem with the seed in thorny ground was that it was "unfruitful'. And really how could it be, with a vice around its nutrient supply.

Slow and Subtle Coiling

In Psalms chapter one we get a synopsis of how this constriction "process" takes place. In telling us what a "blessed man" doesn't do we can see how the snake goes to work in the life of a believer.

A.J. RUBANO, D.C.

Blessed is the man that walketh not in the counsel of the ungodly, nor standeth in the way of sinners, nor sitteth in the seat of the scornful. Psalms 1: 1

Spiritual destruction doesn't happen overnight, it just seems that way. What does occur is a steady slide away from the things of God, and no where do we get a clearer picture of that than in this one verse. Notice that it begins with the walk.

I see this all the time in my practice. Someone walks (or crawls) in to my office complaining of pain that started out innocently enough, but escalated into something much worse. When injury occurred instead of getting the attention their condition warranted they took the advice of their brother's sister's aunt's friend who had something similar a few years ago. *Sometimes a little knowledge can do a lot of damage.* I've seen people get extremely ill after taking some one else's prescription pain medication to the point where all I could do was call for an ambulance. I have also witnessed the damaging effects of treatment rendered by an untrained friend or spouse who thought that providing an adjustment to the spine was just getting the body to "crack."

And so it is with the choking effect of the enemy. It starts with a little well meaning advice from someone who doesn't have the heart of God. That is what an ungodly person is. I know you were thinking the devil and the pitch fork and that is what he would like you to think too. Remember, though, we are instructed that the devil masquerades as an angel of light. The ungodly are those who readily mix the ways of the world with some truth, so long as it doesn't interfere with their fun. So, while you are walking the walk of a believer, the snake slips you a "mickey" through someone you respect who has worldly wisdom. They feed you little things that don't seem so wrong, ideals that you can justify in your head. If you think on those things, like say cheating on your taxes or wondering what it would be like to be single again, long enough they won't even seem wrong after a while. Then the snake can get you to stand around…..

Once the snake gets its coils around you it will want to tighten the grip making it more difficult for you to get out of his grasp. After a time of giving in to the voice of the ungodly it becomes that much easier to "stand in the way" of sinners. Instead of moving forward in your faith you stagnate. You become stuck with one foot in heaven and one foot in the world. Single thoughts and words now become mindsets and fantasies that develop into strongholds. The sinner is one who will do things contrary to the will of God and not even give it a second thought because to them sin is not wrong, *its fun.* They figure they are not hurting anybody, so what is the big deal. (Of course we know the big deal is they are hurting themselves both now and in the world to come). As you stand around with the sinner, in *"his way"* you will be sucked into *"his world."* We are not supposed to hang around sinners. We are supposed to impact their lives for Jesus. So if you're thinking about justifying your relationship with sinners by saying "Jesus hung around sinners and publicans" remember that in those situations Jesus was the one doing the talking and steering them right into God's arms. If you are not doing that then the snake is getting you into the sitting posture……

The scornful ones are those who literally point the finger at God and blame Him for all that ails the world or deny His existence all together. Now, no longer moving forward, and not even standing still, but going backwards. Let me tell you it is a sad thing to see a person who once proclaimed Jesus as Lord come to the point where they say they are so angry at God and so cold that they will no longer serve Him, like a corpse laying breathless after experiencing the death grip of a constrictor.

It's Not How You Start

In the world of professional athletics the men who play the game are largely judged on the numbers they produce. When we think about sports we are drawn to extraordinary careers and single game performances. That's why players like Hank Aaron, the baseball homerun king, Wayne Gretzky known as the "Great One" in hockey circles and Wilt Chamberlain, the only man to ever score one hundred points in a single NBA game are remembered.

In the 2006-2007 NBA season one team, the New Jersey Nets accomplished something no team had ever done before. This record, though, is one this team filled with All-Stars would like to forget. The Nets were facing the Chicago Bulls, noted more for their youth than anything else, and quickly found holes in the Chicago defense. The Nets opened up an eighteen point lead, before the Bulls had even scored a single point. That's right; when the Nets coach, Lawrence Frank looked up at the scoreboard, just a few minutes into the contest the scoreboard read NETS 18 BULLS 0.

It's How You Finish That Counts

The only problem, it was all down hill from there, as the Nets turned the ball over, committed ill advised fouls, and suddenly lost the ability to put the ball in the basket. Ultimately, the Nets lost not only the lead but eventually the game to a team many experts considered inferior to their squad.

The Net's story is not unlike that of King Uzziah, who became king of Judah at the age of sixteen. The bible tells us that King Uzziah started off strong in the Lord.

Sixteen years old was Uzziah when he began to reign, and he reigned fifty and two years in Jerusalem. His mother's name also was Jecoliah of Jerusalem. And he did that which was right in the sight of the LORD, according to all that his father Amaziah did. II Chronicles 26:3-4

His secret was that he sought the Lord, and as long as he did that he was successful.

And he sought God in the days of Zechariah, who had understanding in the visions of God: and as long as he sought the LORD, God made him to prosper. II Chronicles 26:5

Unfortunately for Uzziah he responded to prosperity in much the same way many of the Kings before him and those that followed his reign. Uzziah got wrapped up in the task of developing a military super-power. He engaged in the design, manufacture, and stockpile of weapons. Uzziah succumbed to the pursuit of riches and power and the cares of this world, and ultimately had the life giving word of God choked out of him....by his own choices.

And Uzziah prepared for them throughout all the host shields, and spears, and helmets, and habergeons, and bows, and slings to cast stones. And he made in Jerusalem engines, invented by cunning men, to be on the

towers and upon the bulwarks, to shoot arrows and great stones withal. And his name spread far abroad; for he was marvelously helped, till he was strong. <u>But when he was strong, his heart was lifted up to his destruction: for he transgressed against the LORD his God</u>, and went into the temple of the LORD to burn incense upon the altar of incense. II Chronicles 26:14-16

Uzziah opened the door for sin to lead to his ultimate destruction. The more his fame spread, the tighter the grip of the enemy. The more he focused on the wrong things, the further he got from the right thing, his connection to God. He died a leper.

Uzziah started strong, but finished poorly. The sad thing is, Uzziah's story is all too common in the household of faith. You've seen it happen, a young man gets radically set free, saved, filled with the Holy Spirit. A house of fire for the Lord, he declares I am going to preach the gospel to millions, I am going to pastor a church, God can count on me, I am with you all the way Pastor, I am with you all the way Jesus. And he goes on, and then as quickly and as radically as his life is set on course he is gone. No, it is not at all how you begin, its how you finish this race that matters.

The God of the Second Chance

Fortunately, God is in the business of the second chance, if the snake has his coils around you, shake him off. In the area of getting caught up in your own successes and your own strength in such a way that you lose sight of the Lord in your life, you shake off the snake by realizing and bringing to your remembrance that it is not by your might, it's not by your power, but it is by His Spirit declares the Lord. Your success is directly tied to your link to the Spirit of God.

Don't Be Defeated By Discouragement

Perhaps the most common area today, where the enemy has attempted to crush believers is through the constrictive process of discouragement. Most people have little problem getting excited about something for a few days, or even a couple of weeks; but what happens when the first sign of opposition arises? What happens when the initial state of euphoria is gone? What happens when the first sign of trouble comes your way?

As I said before if the enemy realizes he can't beat you by getting you to fall into outright rebellious and sinful behavior, his next step is to try to get you to defeat yourself. It is a sad and unfortunately not uncommon thing for believers to get discouraged. It's no wonder Jesus warned "in this world you will have tribulation". (John 16:33)

Tough times, difficult situations, betrayal, disappointments, and loss are bound to come our way for as long as we walk around in these earth suits God gave us. I have known many instances myself where it seemed like that was all I kept seeing. Like a roller-coaster as I came out of one rough stretch I barely had enough time to gather myself before something else came right at me. The car breaks down unexpectedly, the children all get sick…at the same time, a customer stiffs me on a bill, and the bank realizes it made a mistake and reports that back interest owed on a loan is due NOW. The list goes on and on, and I am sure you have your own list or two or three.

But let me give you a little bit of encouragement a friend of mine shared with me during a time when I was struggling personally enduring a separation from my wife due to career related circumstances, and he certainly had every reason to respond like Job's wife and say curse God and die.

Allow me to put this in context for you. My friend had had a career as a pro baseball player, a motivational speaker, and as a very successful marketing consultant. He worked with the likes of Jack Nickalaus, Arnold Palmer, and Marilyn McCoo of Fifth Dimension fame. He had enjoyed a great deal of success in everything he did and he was now at a point in his life where all at once it seemed like it was crashing down. His wife had become seriously ill and as a result of all the energy that was needed to properly care for her and get her the best medical attention and nutrition possible he was not available to focus on his business as it needed to be tended to. His business soon began to fail, as he lost several large contracts.

Needless to say my friend was in dire straits, to top it off his teenage son began to act out in the anger that often accompanies an unexpected loss. He was not only seeing his mother dying, but had lost the attention of his parents that he desperately needed at this very critical point in his life. Nothing like piling on! Now I have been through some difficult situations, but I would be lying to you if I told you I knew what this man was going through. I can only imagine the vice like grip around his body and the sheer frustration and emotion he was experiencing.

A Lesson in the Cards

Now I want you to listen to what he told me during this time of his life that helped lift me. He said "A.J.". "I don't know if you have ever played cards", to which I responded

78

with a shake of my head, yes (not that I was any good and never for anything other than to pass time). "In the game of cards the very successful players know how to do something called counting cards, the better you are at counting cards, the more likely you are to know the percentages of what cards your opponents have compared to what you have and therefore the better you become at decision making." He looked at me straight in the face and said, "I am not a great card counter, but one thing I or anyone who has even very little experience playing cards can tell you is that there are only 4 Aces in the deck." He said when I know I've got all four aces, or that all four aces have passed through the deck I am not concerned by someone who is bluffing as if they have the deck's fifth Ace."

I know when the enemy is trying to make it look like everything is going against me it's a lie because I've already got the deck in my favor. All he is doing is trying to create a smoke screen, a diversion if you will to get me to take my eyes of Jesus and focus on the problems. My situation may not change right away, but you know what, I serve a God who never changes. Jesus Christ the same yesterday, today, and for ever (Hebrews 13:7-9) is not about to let you be defeated by a foe he already defeated on your behalf.

He won't change, his promises don't change. He has given us his word to change you and me. He has filled us with His power to overcome ANY situation or circumstance that comes our way. That's His will for us.

> JESUS WON'T CHANGE, HIS PROMISES DON'T CHANGE. HE HAS GIVEN US HIS WORD TO CHANGE YOU AND ME.

And be not conformed to this world: but be ye transformed by the renewing of your mind, that ye may prove what is that good, and acceptable, and perfect, will of God. (Romans 12:2)

No, He doesn't shift or turn, and your situation and circumstance may not change when or how you want it to, but He is instructing you to change the way you think about the circumstances, the way you think about yourself and your ability to overcome, the way you think about how your God thinks about you and what He wants to do in you and through you to make you able to rise over and above the circumstance.

Look Out For Discouragement's Twin Brother

When I was a kid I had a friend named Esteban who was a pretty accomplished athlete. You name the sport and he was probably regarded as the best in the neighborhood at it. He was a natural in soccer, and although he had perhaps the worst basketball shooting form you'd ever see he had an uncanny ability to put the ball in the hoop. It wasn't pretty, but it was effective. The thing about Esteban is that, no matter how good he was, you didn't always want him on your team. "The reason?" you ask. Wherever Esteban went, so went his little, much less athletic, younger brother Tony. So if you picked Esteban, you got Tony as part of a packaged deal.

If discouragement had a sibling I believe his name would be Frustration. The two are closely linked together and one usually follows the other. You try something, you are persistent at it, you've read all the books, studied all the relevant material and yet the end results don't change. It happens to people from all walks of life, CEO's, teachers, politicians, star athletes, and maybe even, YOU.

Someone once defined *insanity* as doing the same thing over and over again and expecting a different result. When it comes to *frustration* a viable definition is trying different things over and over and getting the same result.

Doing the wrong thing over and over again and expecting something good *is* crazy. But what if you actually are on the right track and you haven't seen the desired results yet, does that mean you should all of a sudden switch to something else, a new routine. Different, isn't always better.

The Power of Combination

If you have ever struggled to meet your potential, it may not be because you are not on the right course. Sometimes, probably more often than you would anticipate, people who are headed in the right direction but have not yet seen their goals fulfilled get discouraged and frustrated and decide to try something "different". You know the saying, if you are doing the same thing over and over and expecting a different result you are the definition of insanity. The problem is that they just drop what they were doing and try something totally new, when all they *really* needed to do was *add* one other habit or discipline to what they were already doing to see their efforts produce the fruit they desired. Listen to this story of one of sports all time greats and see if you can get a feel for what I am talking about.

Michael Jordan is regarded by many as being the greatest basketball player of all time. He tantalized spectators with his high flying court acrobatics, literally flying through the air in effortless fashion before throwing down a dunk. Cut by his high school basketball coach he worked his way to a college scholarship and, as a freshman, at the University of North Carolina led an all star laden team to the 1984 National Championship Victory.

When Jordan entered the NBA as the third overall pick the following year expectations were high from the team that drafted him, the Chicago Bulls, as well as the rabid NBA fans who had seen his meteoric rise in college. But a funny thing happened to Michael Jordan on his way to becoming, arguably, the NBA's greatest player............

You see, although Jordan put up great statistical numbers in points and lit up the highlight reels with his breathtaking dunks he had yet to fulfill the goal that the Bulls and their fans had set....winning an NBA championship. After seven years in the league, two slam dunk titles, five NBA scoring titles, and six all star game appearances Jordan was referred to as a selfish player who could not win the ultimate prize.

Change Is Coming

All of that changed when the Bulls added one key component to their team. As great as Jordan was he still could not do it all on his own. If the Bulls were to ever win that elusive title he needed someone who could complement his abilities on the court. That person, for Michael Jordan, was Scottie Pippen. Pippen was a great defender, with excellent speed, and the willingness to subject his talents and take on the supporting role to Jordan's lead. The rest is, of course, history as the Jordan/Pippen led Bulls went on to win six NBA Championships and thus seal the place in history for not only Michael, but Scottie as well.

SHAKE OFF THE SNAKE

The Definition of Frustration

Doing the same thing over and over and expecting a different result is insanity, BUT, constantly changing what you are doing and still getting the same result will drive you to frustration. No where do I see people struggle with this more so than in their finances. Changing jobs frequently, coming up with get rich quick schemes, trying overly risky investments can work to improve your financial standing, but all too often are the cause of frustration and discouragement. People come up to me and tell me they tried tithing, some for years, without seeing the results that the Bible promises. They ask me, "Why are the windows of heaven not opening up for me?" In many of these situations the "solution" is to say "tithing doesn't work" and then, they make the biggest financial mistake of their lives and stop (tithing).

Add a *Second* Skill or Discipline

In Acts chapter ten we are given one of the greatest secrets of prosperity known to man. It is something I like to call the power of combination. To be successful at anything in life you have to be able to do at least ONE THING extremely well. Maybe your forte is baking, or speaking in public. Perhaps you are great with numbers, have a knack for managing people well, or are really good at organizing things. Whatever it is, you are really good at that ONE THING. But imagine for a moment how much your effectiveness would improve if you added a second, complimentary skill. You could now take your baking business to the next level by having an organized method for tracking which parts of the country like pecan pie instead of apple cobbler. If you are a bookworm who developed some better people skills you could network and get even more clients for your book-keeping business; whatever the combination, acquiring that second skill DOES NOT mean giving up the first. On the contrary it serves to enhance your greatest strength. And don't be fooled, not everyone is born with the skills you see them excelling at. Remember, Michael Jordan was CUT from his high school basketball team. You can develop just about every skill, from sales and marketing to speaking and more technical skills like accounting.

What Works in the Spiritual Works in the Natural

I have seen this type of turn around played out over and over again in my practice with patients who jumped from doctor to doctor, and therapy to therapy. Once they realized that they could benefit by integrated different approaches. Sometimes Chiropractic by itself was not enough, but once we added nutritional supplements or had them under-go a course of physical therapy to strengthen their joints and muscles the results came and their overall experience was enhanced. It wasn't that one approach was wrong it just needed a second or in some cases third complimentary approach for that person to flourish.

Get God's Attention

So, in Acts chapter ten we see the story of a gentile (non-Jew) named Cornelius who loved God and loved the Jewish people. Up until this point in time the Gentiles were considered outsiders to the Kingdom of God, at least to the powers that be in the early church (remember Jesus death on the cross had already cleared the way). Cornelius though got the attention of God, and as a result his family and the church will never be the same.

There was a certain man in Caesarea called Cornelius, a centurion of the band called the Italian band, A devout man, and one that feared God with all his house, which *gave much alms* to the people, and *prayed to God alway*. He saw in a vision evidently about the ninth hour of the day an angel of God coming in to him, and saying unto him, Cornelius. And when he looked on him, he was afraid, and said, What is it, Lord? And he said unto him, *Thy prayers and thine alms are come up for a memorial before God.* Acts 10:1-4 (italics added)

Cornelius combined the action of giving, (the Bible says he gave "much" alms to the poor) with the fervency of prayer (prayed to God always) and as a result he grabbed a hold of God's heart strings. When it comes to our finances we must understand that it is God's good pleasure to pour blessings on us provided our motives are right, provided he can count on us to be a funnel of blessing to the world. The scripture tells us to ask in faith not wavering, to delight ourselves in HIM and he will give us the desires of our heart (Psalm37:4). The answer to your financial stress is NEVER to stop giving, but actually to increase it, AND bathe your giving in prayers and requests in behalf of the needs of others. Don't stop doing what you are already doing just add that second discipline, that second successful habit and you will see INCREASE! The answer to your health struggles may mean you need to combine good eating with exercise, just because you tried one or the other without success doesn't mean you weren't on the right path.

> **DON'T STOP DOING WHAT YOU ARE
> ALREADY DOING JUST ADD THAT SECOND
> DISCIPLINE, THAT SECOND SUCCESSFUL
> HABIT AND YOU WILL SEE INCREASE!**

The answer to your employment struggles may mean sending resumes not just by fax, but also by email *and* with a head hunter, in other words don't quit what you were already doing just step it up another notch by ADDING something else.

Don't Ever Give Up

Elijah experienced tremendous frustration to go along with his discouragement in the face of Ahab and Jezebel's pursuit of him and effort to take his life. It struck him so deep that he decided he wanted to beat them to the punch, and have his life ended before they could take it away.

But he himself (Elijah) went a day's journey into the wilderness, and came and sat down under a juniper tree: and he requested for himself that he might die; and said, It is enough; now, O LORD, take away my life; for I am not better than my fathers. (I Kings 19:4)

It saddens me when I think of the people of God who sit in this same predicament actually wanting God to end their life. Some go so far as to actually take matters into their own hands. It touches me close to home, because I was there. Newly saved, yet frustrated by events and discouraged by situations in my life I actually came to the place where I prayed for God to take my life, and then tried, unsuccessfully to do it myself.

I look at what God has done through me and all that he has given me since and to think I almost threw all that away- because I didn't see his plan right in front of me. If you are in that place right now, let me encourage you to STOP!! You think your problem is too great.... It Is. You think you can't make it alone.... You can't. You think you don't have the strength to overcome..... You don't. But look at what God had for Elijah and take heart.....

And as he lay and slept under a juniper tree, behold, then an angel touched him, and said unto him, Arise and eat. And he looked, and, behold, there was a cake baken on the coals, and a cruse of water at his head. And he did eat and drink, and laid him down again. And the angel of the LORD came again the second time, and touched him, and said, Arise and eat; because the journey is too great for thee. And he arose, and did eat and drink, and went in the strength of that meat forty days and forty nights unto Horeb the mount of God. (I Kings 19-5-8)

You are not going to figure this thing out on your own, but the Spirit of God knows what you need. If you are going to shake of the constriction of the snake the Word of God has got to course through your very being, as it did here for Elijah sustaining him until such time came as he was able to hear God in that still small voice.

It Can and Does Happen To the Best of Us

One of the things that I find holds so many people with tremendous talent and ability back is when they look at someone who has already crossed the bridge of success in life with the thought that the successful person has been that way forever. The mindset that the successful person was born with some sort of silver spoon in their mouth and had everything handed to them on a silver platter.

> ONE THING YOU WILL FIND THAT MOST SUCCESSFUL PEOPLE HAVE IN COMMON IS THAT THEY HAVE IN FACT BEEN THROUGH TIMES IN THEIR LIFE OF EITHER GREAT TRIALS OR GREAT DISCOURAGEMENT AND COME OUT THE OTHER SIDE.

Let me share a little secret with you. Come real close and listen to this because I am only going to say this once.

That is ABSOLUTELY NOT TRUE.

In fact one thing you will find that most successful people have in common is that they have, in fact, been through times in their life of either great trials or great discouragement and come out the other side. Read about someone like Tony Robbins the great motivational speaker and entrepreneur and you will see that he was literally broke, busted, and disgusted before he launched his program that has now helped literally millions of people tap into the "Giant Within".

The Great Ones Didn't Always Look So Great

Can you imagine Tony Robbins, fat and out of shape, eating pork and beans out of a can, sitting in a one bedroom efficiency with a beat up old car, thousands of dollars in credit card debt and....jobless. Imagine it, 'cause it happened

The same can be said for Oprah, Condoleezza Rice, and Colin Powell. These are great men and women who have overcome fear, discouragement, hard luck, or whatever you want to call it. So don't think for one minute you have a corner on the market of frustration and discouragement.

That being said you are unique such that no one responds just as you do to the circumstances in your life the way you do. You have got to reach into your uniqueness and understand that God wants to use that for his glory. By understanding your unique weaknesses you can learn to depend on God's strength in that area. By understanding your unique strengths you can learn to develop those in such a way as to give glory to the Father in your overcoming.

Remember this, the great men and women of faith weren't always that way. Gideon, looked in the mirror and saw a loser. He was the youngest from the least of all the tribes of Israel. Fortunately God saw something different. Moses saw his speech impediment, but God didn't care about that either. Even the Apostle Paul had his thorn to deal with, and yet he fulfilled the destiny God had for him. God didn't make you to fail and he didn't create you to be small in the face of your challenges but to rise above them.

Facing Your Mountains and Giants

In the movie "Facing the Giants" a critical scene in the movie comes about when the star player of this perennial losing football team makes a comment about the strength of the team's upcoming opponent and how his team had very little chance of winning this game. The attitude and future success of the team takes a dramatic turn for the better when the coach confronts this star player and puts him to an unusual test.

Do Your *Very* Best

The coach, who is a new coach to this team, challenges this star player to go farther than he ever had gone before in a strength drill. In this particular drill a player carries another player on his back while crawling on his hands and feet (knees and elbows are not permitted to touch the ground).

You Have Yet to Tap Into Your Ability

The player accepts the challenge and suggests that perhaps he can go *thirty* yards, which would be *ten* yards farther, fifty percent more than he had ever done before. The coach, though, had other plans, he could see the potential in this young man and he knew he hadn't even scratched the surface. He had grown up with this team losing, and losing has a way of infecting all that we do. Before playing at this school he had known nothing but success, but now it was different, now he had hung around and gotten used to losing. He didn't come out and say, "I am a loser" or put one of those "L"'s on his forehead, but he had bought into what it takes to be a loser. He no longer put out the extra effort, that little something that separates the mediocre from the great, the winner from the loser. Let me suggest that you can be on the wrong side of the score but still demonstrating the intangibles that make a winner a winner.

So this rookie coach isn't about to accept a fifty percent improvement when he knows this young man can do better. He blindfolds him and tells the young man to promise him he'll give it his very best effort.

In return the coach promises to be a source of encouragement and strength; in short he won't allow the young man to give up on himself.

And so the challenge began with the team's star going easily past the thirty yard barrier he had set up in his head, and as he appeared to fatigue just short of the forty the coach continued to remind him of his promise to give his very best. The star athlete pushed on past the fifty yard, then sixty yard barrier complaining of cramping in his arms and legs. After being reminded by the coach that he hadn't yet emptied himself he pressed on until finally he let his arms and legs drop to the ground, completely exhausted and utterly emptied out, just as he crossed the far goal line, some one-hundred yards away from where he started.

Won't or Can't?

Brother and sister I want you to know Jesus will never be down on you for what you can't do, but He is concerned by what you are not willing to do, where you are not willing to go, and what you are not willing to pursue in your life. The Bible records that Jesus literally emptied himself on our behalf, pouring out everything to save us.

There came a time before his death on the cross when he went away to a quiet place to pray. Most of us know the story recorded about His experience in the Garden of Gesthamane. He brought with Him his top disciples, and found that they couldn't keep watch with him 1 hour before falling asleep.

> JESUS WILL NEVER BE DOWN ON YOU FOR WHAT YOU CAN'T DO, BUT HE IS CONCERNED BY WHAT YOU ARE NOT WILLING TO DO, WHERE YOU ARE NOT WILLING TO GO, AND WHAT YOU ARE NOT WILLING TO PURSUE IN YOUR LIFE.

I find myself in this position frequently when working with people who have a chronic injury or illness. After years of accepting their pain or limitations as normal they begin to reconcile in their mind that they can't get better, when in actuality they have simply chosen not to. Perhaps they are correct in thinking they will never be one hundred percent again, but even if they only got twenty to thirty percent better they would experience a much fuller life. Often I find myself in a position of not doctor, but coach in their life as I show them the difference between their ability and their willingness and encourage them to stretch beyond what their mind *says* they can do to what I know they are capable of doing.

A Lesson from Dating

Isn't it amazing though the things we can do when we really want something. I remember when I courted my wife; it was never a problem for me to stay up to all hours of the night talking with her on the phone, or going to a late movie even after I had just worked ten hours in the summer sun. I think of my children who struggle to get up on Sunday morning for Church, but have no problem jumping out of bed before me on a Saturday to watch their favorite cartoons after staying up beyond midnight Friday. It tells me there is something on the inside of us that can drive us to do more than we think we are capable of.

John Hagee put it like this in his book, "The Seven Secrets of Genuine Greatness", when referring to people who said they couldn't do something that seemed difficult. "If you change the word CAN'T to WON'T at least you have faced the truth." I am inclined to agree with him on that, because my God tells me "I can do all things through Christ (the anointed one and his anointing) which strengthens me." (Philippians 4:13) God is not so much concerned about what you can't do. He has that covered, because anything you are not physically able to accomplish he is able to make His grace abound. God is concerned, however, about what you won't do. As long as you are willing and obedient YOU WILL eat the good of the land. (Is. 1:19)

You *can* face and overcome the snake in your life, through a personal decision and act of your will with the help of the Holy Spirit. Don't be afraid to empty yourself. Jesus proved you could do it, as He underwent the experience of the cross, not as God, not as Jesus the Christ, but as Jesus of Nazareth

Defeating Depression

If we are not careful, and even if we are, discouragement and frustration can lead to depression. Depression is diabolical in that it paralyzes men and women of God because not only is it emotionally draining, it is also physically defeating as well..... and it doesn't have to be.

There are several causes of depression, some are chemical and involve imbalances that science still hasn't completely answered, but most are related to areas under our direct control. Those are the ones I want to deal with.

> TOO MANY TIMES WE'VE CONFUSED
> EMOTIONAL PROBLEMS WITH
> NORMAL EMOTIONS RELEASED
> OVER A THOUGHT PROBLEM.

In this day and age where a high demand and high expectations are being placed on us from childhood depression has been on the rise. Presently nearly twenty percent of Americans suffer from some sort of depression, and treatment for depression is second only to cancer in terms of economic impact costing an estimated forty-four billion dollars per year.

To defeat depression we need the power of the Holy Ghost, yes, and we need to get a handle on what we are *thinking* about. As I said earlier there are biological factors in some people leading to depression, but I have a hard time believing that after hundreds of years all of a sudden some new genetic epidemic of poor body chemistry just sprouted up. It seems much more likely that the demands of day to day life and the lack of control of our mental thought process is more to blame.

Look at these causes of depression:

**Unrealistic Expectations not being fulfilled
Extreme Disappointments
Lack of or poor Self Esteem
Unfair Comparisons**

What do they all have in common? They are all *external factors* exerting a stress on our *internal* thought process. They are *not* chemicals gone awry. If you've been diagnosed with a clinical depression I am not minimizing your pain, but we need to take a realistic look at what it is we are dealing with in this area. Too many times we've confused emotional problems with normal emotions released over a Thought Problem.

Let me explain. If you keep thinking about a loved one that passed away you SHOULD have the emotion of being sad. If you are constantly thinking about a time when someone betrayed your confidence it is NORMAL to be angry or upset. If you are always reflecting on an incident when someone tried to harm you the EXPECTED response would be fear.

All of these are normal and expected human emotions for the *thoughts* going through our mind. Here's the rub, God has instructed us on how to defeat this form of depression by controlling what we think about.....

Finally, brethren, whatsoever things are true, whatsoever things are honest, whatsoever things are just, whatsoever things are pure, whatsoever things are lovely, whatsoever things are of good report; if there be any virtue, and if there be any praise, think on these things. Philippians 4:8

I know what you are going to say, so just hold that thought for a minute. It is *not easy* to change your thinking,

95

BUT you are capable of doing it. How do I know? Because *God is not in the business of commanding His children to do things they can't do.* He wouldn't have told Moses to stand before Pharaoh if He didn't think Moses was able to fulfill his role. He wouldn't have sent angels to find Gideon if He wasn't convinced Gideon could lead the people to victory. Likewise He doesn't command you to do something that you aren't able to do.

Here's your prescription to shake off the snake when it comes to depression, seven things you can start doing NOW to shake off those excess emotions.

Hang with the Eagles

Get around godly people, who are positive. It makes no sense hanging around people, even Christians, who are wet rags, dragging you down and piling more of their problems on top of yours. There are plenty of people who you can find, if you look for them, that have a positive, uplifting word to help guide you and encourage you on your way.

Focus on Good Things

Stop focusing on the bad around you AND start looking for the good in things. It may be cliché, but it helps to stop and smell the roses. Don't read the news articles that talk about death and deception, instead look at the ones that reveal the heart of caring people or the miracle hand of God in action

Control Your Tongue

Mediate on *and* confess the word of God daily. See what God has done through the ages and let His word transform your mind and thought process. The word was sent to us for that reason (Romans 12: 2). Get the word of God in you every day and speak to yourself the promises that relate to your situation. Death and life are in the power of your tongue, so why not let your tongue go to work for you declaring and decreeing the future you want.

Don't put off 'til Tomorrow

Don't procrastinate. According to research a common trait in people who have constantly battled with depression is that of "piling on". Instead of tackling issues or assignments when they arise, they put them off for another day. Get to work NOW on those issues that are at hand, and gradually catch up on the ones that have fallen by the wayside.

Let Go and Let God

Walk in forgiveness. If you are holding something against someone it is time to let it go. Realize that if someone wronged you they have probably long since moved on, if you're holding a grudge it is only enslaving *you*. Let go and let God is the saying that is popularized on bumper stickers and is so appropriate to this situation. Let God fight your battles; let God heal your heart.

A.J. RUBANO, D.C.

Learn the Secret of the "Magic" Mustard Seed

Do something nice for someone else. A story is recounted, in Reverend Brian Cavanaugh's book, *The Sower's Seeds*, about a woman who lost her son in a terrible accident. She went to the priest in her town and asked him if there was something he could do to "magically" bring her son back. The priest instructed her to find a home that had never known sorrow and to obtain from the owner of the house a magic mustard seed and when she had obtained the seed to bring it back to him. The very first house the woman came upon was in a very wealthy neighborhood, it had huge French doors at the entry way, immaculately groomed landscaping, and a huge chandelier in the foyer of the home. When the lady of the house answered the door the woman spoke softly and said I am looking for a home that has known no sorrow, and seeing all the beauty of your dwelling I decided to stop here first. "Is this such a place?" she asked. The lady of the house responded, as tears welled up in her eyes, "I am sorry we do not fit that description" and she began to tell the woman of the recent trials of her life. The woman began to think within herself, who better to comfort this poor family than I who have experienced sadness myself and she stayed several days consoling and comforting the family. She never did find the "magic" mustard seed, but what she did find was far greater as she went from home to home bringing comfort to the hurting.

The times when I have struggled personally with sadness, anger, defeat, or a multitude of emotions running wild taking my eyes off my own problems and focusing on the needs of others has always provided a source of healing and refreshing. Take the time each day to do something nice for someone else.

Get Wet

Drink more water and exercise. Dehydration can and will cause you to have feelings of depression. A two percent reduction in normal cellular hydration levels can lead to a twenty percent decrease in productivity and mental acuity. In this fast food age where taste and flavor take such a high value in our lives water is replaced in our diet by soda, fancy iced tea, and a multitude of energy drinks. Your increased energy levels in the absence of proper water intake can cause not only your skin, but your emotions to droop. Ideally half your body weight in water is sufficient unless you work or play in extreme temperatures. (Example 200 lb = 100 oz. of water) Just twenty minutes of exercise three to four times per week will help change you hormonally in such a way as to spark more energy and feel better about yourself. Remember, exercise, even if it only "profits a little," still profits you.

When people come to me for a physical problem that has affected their ability to enjoy the activities of life for any length of time there is almost always and emotional backlash. Sometimes before I can get them to feel better physically I have got to get them to realize first and foremost that they can get better. One prescription that works great and also has functioned as an indicator of how much compliance I can expect in the person's care is to double their present water intake and get them to walk just ten minutes three times per week. In almost every case, without fail, I see an immediate up turn in the patient's overall outlook.

Be Enthusiastic

En theos, the root word for enthusiastic means God

Within. As you let God live through you the blues just can't. Why else would we be encouraged that "The Joy of the Lord is our strength." (Nehemiah 8:10)

Find out what it is that gets and keeps you fired up and focused and use it to your advantage. Maybe it is a certain type of music (stay away from the sad songs!!!!), or a specific kind of lighting (natural vs. artificial). Think about the people that motivate you and listen to them on your way to work or at work if that is acceptable. If you're a sports fan try playing clips of your teams greatest victories (I once made a video montage of Yankee playoff clinching victories). Be creative and keep your relationship with Jesus at the heart of your efforts.

"FAITH IS NOT THE DENIAL OF
CIRCUMSTANCES, RATHER THE
DENIAL OF THE RIGHT FOR
THOSE CIRCUMSTANCES TO
RULE OVER YOUR LIFE."

DR. DAVID T DEMOLA

"WHEN YOU SEE A RATTLESNAKE
POISED TO STRIKE YOU, DON'T
WAIT UNTIL HE HAS STRUCK
BEFORE YOU CRUSH HIM."

FRANKLIN D ROOSEVELT

CHAPTER 6

SNAKE BIT: SIGNS AND SYMPTOMS

"Pain is temporary. It may last a minute, or an hour, or a day, or a year, but eventually it will subside and something else will take its place. If I quit, however, it lasts forever."

Lance Armstrong, 7 time Tour de France Winner

According to the Palm Beach County (FL) Herpetological Society there are approximately seven-thousand recorded snake bites each year in the United States. The majority of snake bites are inflicted below the knee. One thing we know for sure is that the enemy doesn't play by the rules. He will definitely strike below the belt when given the opportunity.

The study goes on to report that of the bites that occur over half do not result in venom being injected, and death results in *only* one in five hundred cases. To tell you the truth I wouldn't care if it was one in five million, I don't want to be a pin cushion for any snake, poisonous or not.

With that being said when a snake strikes in the natural you would be hard pressed to find a recipient who didn't know they had been bitten. Of course there would be the obvious sign of blood and a quick, sharp prick. Determining whether the bite was from a venomous species, on the other hand, might be a little bit more difficult to detect immediately. Despite what you may have been taught about the appearance of deadly species, poisonous snakes come in all sizes and color schemes.

In the spirit and soul realm detecting the bite and its effects are no less critical to your ability to getting the attention your affliction requires than it is for an outdoorsman stung by the venom of a rattler, cobra, or black mamba out in the wild. Speed and precision are necessary to preventing or limiting the long lasting consequences that can result from prolonged exposure to the poison.

Here is what you need to look out for when the enemy rears its ugly head.

Severe Localized Pain

When the enemy bites it hurts. It is painful to be betrayed, lied to, cheated on, to be physically ill, or emotionally battered. It hurts when your dreams of success appear to be shattered, when you can't figure out where to turn in the area of your finances, or when you lose a loved one. Pretending these things are not hurtful doesn't make you any more or less spiritual. If I heard my pastor say it once I have heard it a thousand times, and even so it is no less powerful. Faith is *not* the denial of circumstances.

If you are bitten by a snake and try to act like it didn't hurt the only one you are fooling is yourself. When I was separated from my wife it was worse than any injury I had ever suffered at any point in my life. I often tell people it was akin to undergoing heart surgery without the benefit of anesthesia. I experienced a plethora of negative emotions from feelings of failure, to anger, and then a host of "what-ifs" and "if-onlys". What if I had said the right words? What if I was more sensitive to my wife's emotions? If only I hadn't lost my temper?

For a while I tried to act like everything was fine, and pushed away all of my friends' attempts to help me. Trying to hide the pain didn't do anything to resolve the problems I faced, and neither will it for you. If anything my efforts to subvert my agony made matters worse. Let me explain.

In my practice I am frequently in the position of having to tell a patient the reason why the best thing for an injury isn't always to remove the pain; especially in instances when I am working with athletes or people who are very active. I have found that people who are always on the go do not want to stop for anything. When pain hits, their first instinct is not usually to rest and deal with the source of discomfort but instead to take a pain killer to deaden the sense of agony. No wonder addictions to prescription medications are fast becoming a national concern and will soon outweigh usage of illegal narcotics.

Addictions to prescription medication are not the only detrimental effect I want to shield my patients from; in fact, though I am extremely cognizant of the potential for misuse, it is relatively low on the totem pole of my thinking. A more prevalent concern is that by "masking" the outward symptom of pain with either an over the counter product or a prescription analgesic the people I care for will either aggravate the present injury or make themselves more susceptible to further complicating the problem. I recall a baseball player under my care that came to see me after an improperly treated back problem led to arm trouble. Through the use of corticosteroids the back problem apparently went away, allowing him to continue to pitch with altered mechanics. In other words he still pitched but was forced to change his normal motion to do so. Repeated throwing with the new delivery put additional stress on his arm until he experienced a loud pop in his shoulder followed by severe pain in his shoulder joint and upper arm. Fortunately he hadn't torn any ligaments, even though the resultant strain on his arm would keep him out of action for two to four weeks. Had he sought my care initially and taken a short time of rest from the back problem he most likely would have avoided a long stay on the disabled list.

Don't Disconnect the Alarm

Let me put it to you this way. If the fire alarm in my home began to ring incessantly as the result of an actual fire you would think I was pretty dumb if, instead of dealing with the flames, I took the battery out of the alarm to save my ears from the annoyance. Both steps will stop the buzzing, but the latter will allow the fire to continue to burn, prevent or slow the arrival of trained fire fighters, and lead to severe fiscal and physical consequences.

When the enemy stings you let the pain lead you to the people who can help. Don't try to "mask" it by putting on a false face or pretending it's not there so that everyone *thinks* you are alright. So many times I have seen people, when they need it the most, shy away from the house and people of God in response to their pain because they expect judgment or they fear looking weak. If it is not a hospital for the hurting what is the Church of Jesus Christ? Faith is not a denial of circumstances, just a denial of their right to rule your life. Dealing with pain, the right way, is sometimes part of the process.

Swelling

In medical texts inflammation is defined as a defensive response of the body to stress due to tissue damage characterized by redness, pain, heat, and swelling. Swelling results as proteins in the blood work to form a thick network, called fibrin, to trap and prevent the spread of an invader, like a snake toxin. The body continues the process of "walling off" the area of attack to prevent spread of the damaging substance and works to destroy the venom by mobilizing specialized cells to perform a process called *phagocytosis*, literally eating the waste products. Ultimately pus forms as the mixture of living and non living debris piles up in the tissue underneath the skin. This may last for a few days or even several weeks.

When the viper latched onto Paul this physical response is exactly what the people of Malta expected to take place. Living on an island inhabited by venomous snakes it would seem a certainty that the natives had seen this happen on multiple occasions.

But Paul shook the snake off into the fire and suffered no ill effects. <u>The people expected him to swell up or suddenly fall dead</u>........ Acts 28:5-6

Paul experienced supernatural protection from the bite of this deadly snake, and yes that protection is available to us as believers, but do not discount the sign of swelling. God is the God of the miraculous *and* He is the God of the process. There are things that He brings to pass instantly in our lives and others that require the culmination of a period of time. Failing to submit to the process will cause you to miss out totally or extend your time in it.

> GOD IS THE GOD OF THE MIRACULOUS
> *AND* HE IS THE GOD OF THE PROCESS.
> THERE ARE THINGS THAT HE BRINGS TO
> PASS INSTANTLY IN OUR LIVES AND
> OTHERS THAT REQUIRE THE
> CULMINATION OF A PERIOD OF TIME.

As tissues in the body swell, it is common to experience a different quality of pain in areas where it seemed pain had come and gone, or had begun to subside. One of the types of protein that the immune system releases to combat toxic intruders in the inflammatory response we discussed earlier is called a *defensin.* As its name would suggest it pours in to affected regions to defend against the efforts of poisons to establish a stronghold in your body. It is literally a cellular battle of good versus evil. In your life you may have times where as you attempt to fill your life with new thoughts and a positive outlook on things some of those old, unhealthy emotions and worldly ways of responding will pop up to the surface to reclaim their hold on you.

Rest assured it is normal to struggle with these conflicting feelings. It is how you handle them that will make the difference and determine your success. It is at this point that you have a choice to make. You can give in to the old man or you can allow the godly influences that have been positioned in your life to crowd out and expel the old way of doing things. You can be transformed by the renewing of your mind through the word (Romans 12:2).

SHAKE OFF THE SNAKE

Bruising

In medical terminology a bruise is commonly referred to as a contusion. While bruising to the brain, or what is called a cerebral contusion can be life altering, most cases of external bruising are typically non life threatening; yet, depending on the size and degree of discoloration in the affected area can be the cause of great alarm.

Unfortunately, in the church today I have found that there are too many who could be classified as spiritual hemophiliacs. Instead of just a localized wound, their injury turns into a case of severe and uncontrollable internal bleeding. At the first sign of trouble or offense they are ready to call it quits; willing to allow the enemy to gain a foothold because of a bruised ego.

No Need for Surgery

According to herpetologist, experts in the field of snake study, eighty-five percent of all snake bites take place below the knee. That is an interesting finding, but of no surprise to God by any means. As a matter of fact he prophesied it would be so.

And I will put enmity between thee and the woman, and between thy seed and her seed; it shall bruise thy head, <u>and thou shalt bruise his heel</u>. (God speaking to the serpent in Genesis 3:15)

We shouldn't be caught off guard either when the enemy takes an unfair swipe at us. We also need to take care of bruises like they ought to be treated. Not by requesting major surgery when all we need is an ice pack. Minimizing severe trauma is never wise, but making too much out of a minor event is just as unhealthy.

As a physician I have treated patients who after experiencing a slight neck sprain respond as if they herniated a disc. They may want certain test performed, or specific medications prescribed because of what they perceive to be naturally unalterable pain. As part of my professional responsibility I have to help them see that what they are going through *will* be short lived, and that by not "babying" their body they will actually heal much quicker.

I am convinced that in most cases where people have had their feelings hurt by another believer or someone on the ministry staff at their church there is a simple lack of communication that blows up into a big misunderstanding. It is amazing, though, how the enemy can use mere delusion to break up not only relationships, but whole church bodies as well.

> WHEN SOMEONE OFFENDS YOU SPEAK TO THEM ABOUT IT. INSTEAD OF TELLING EVERYONE ELSE *BUT* THE PERSON WHO HURT YOU, GO DIRECTLY TO THE SOURCE AND GET THE FACTS.

Learn to recognize those surface injuries, and treat them as such, to avoid the destructive consequences the snake hopes will ensue. When someone offends you speak to them about it. Instead of telling everyone else *but* the person who hurt you, go directly to the source and get the facts. Don't think the worst, expect the best from your brother or sister and give them the benefit of the doubt before passing judgment. If there is something more than a misunderstanding then take the concern to your pastor or a leader you trust to see if a resolution befitting family members can take place.

And remember, though it may sting a little that bruise is not fatal.

Blurred Vision

And it shall come to pass afterward, that I will pour out my spirit upon all flesh; and your sons and your daughters shall prophesy, your old men shall dream dreams, your young men shall see visions….. Joel 2: 28

What happens to snake bit people when some of the enemy's toxins seep into their blood stream? They get distorted vision. Instead of clearly seeing the plan of God at work in their life and proclaiming his will for the encouragement of others their eye sight is broadened beyond focus.

Distracted by the ancillary and unimportant they miss the move of the Spirit because they choose to pay attention to what kind of car the pastor is driving or the suit he is wearing. They are disgruntled about the size of the church or the fact someone sat in their favorite seat; bothered by the preaching and teaching on giving, and unsettled because of the sister in the front who keeps shouting "Amen" too loud for their liking. Their eyes hone in on what everyone else is doing wrong or all the things taking place in the "ministry' that seem unfair as if that has anything to do with their personal relationship to God.

In some cases the visual field is so narrowed that it could best be classified as tunnel vision, and what becomes blurred is the delineation between right and wrong. For everyone else there is a black and white set of rules, but once the issues or problems relate to me there is now all of a sudden an area of gray; justified with the phrase "God knows my heart." That's exactly what I am afraid of.

Eye (I) Light Up My Life

The lantern of thy body is thine eye; if thine eye be simple, all thy body shall be light-full; but if thine eye be wayward, all thy body shall be dark[-full]. If then the light that is in thee be darknesses, how great shall those darknesses be? [but if thine eye be wayward, all thy body shall be dark-full. Therefore if the light that is in thee be darkness, how great shall those darknesses be?] Luke 6:22-23 Wycliffe New Testament

When you've been hurt the natural tendency is to distrust, to look at everything and everyone with an eye of skepticism. Some of my closest relationships have been with people who at one time or another said they would not let anyone penetrate their wall. As long as that wall was up they couldn't really give love or receive love, and in their mind they were alright with that, because at least they weren't being actively hurt by the actions of someone else.

I say actively, because we both know the truth. They were still hurting, and bad. Hurting because they needed the love of another and suffering greater damage because they were shutting out the words that were meant to give life, hope, and shed abroad in their hearts the love of God that is in Christ Jesus. Once you allow the light of God's word to penetrate and fill your heart all those dark areas on the inside will be lit up as well.

This applies to every area of your life. When you allowed your eyes to see clearly the message on salvation you were justified and cleansed from all unrighteousness. When you open your eyes to God's word on healing you let healing flow to your heart and physical body. When you widen your perspective to include the truth about God's word for your finances you will prosper in that area.

You do want to prosper? Don't you? Well, to do that you have got to take your focus off everyone else and accept responsibility for you.

.....first cast out the beam out of thine own eye; and then shalt thou see clearly to cast out the mote out of thy brother's eye. Matthew 7: 5

Shock

After the devastation that took place in New York City, Washington D.C., and in the airways over our country on September 11, 2001 one word can best describe the state of the citizens throughout the United States. Shock. It seemed as if we were all party to some ill-conceived joke and were somehow waiting to wake up from a nightmare but the alarm would not go off. Shock can be caused by a vast array of trauma, including a *non-poisonous* snake bite, and is characterized by changes in the heart and breathing rate (elevated in the early stages), clammy and pale skin, hypotension (low blood pressure), and as the brain is affected confusion and loss of consciousness.

The events of that day left many in a stupefied state, wandering around in terror; mouths hanging open in disbe-

A.J. RUBANO, D.C.

lief, rigid, staring blankly into nothingness. What I see today is eerily similar. In the wake of a national economic downturn shock waves have resonated and I have witnessed many of our brothers and sisters in Christ succumb to the effects.

The strategy used in 9/11 and the devices employed against believers and potential new converts alike are one in the same. Recall your emotions as not one, but two jumbo jets crashed into Tower One and then Tower Two only to hear a short time later that the Pentagon had suffered a breach and another plane had been hijacked and headed for the White House before a group of courageous passengers thwarted the plot and lost their lives in the process. Each event was calculated to raise the level of fear and dread to paralyze the American people.

If you have personally experienced simultaneous attacks in more than one area of your life you know exactly what I am talking about. I am talking about more than just a leaky faucet, or some car trouble, but real pressure on your relationships, finances, health, and things that cause you to question your faith. After fighting to overcome it all you experienced a system overload, or full shut down.

First Steps to Treating Shock

During my training at Life University I was instructed in emergency life saving and CPR. As part of that education we were taught to recognize the signs of shock and to treat it as a serious medical condition, understanding that it is more than just an emotional reaction to a traumatic event. The key in preventing permanent damage or death is early intervention and of primary concern is to maintain a stable core body temperature. When patients ask me what they should do if a loved one goes into shock, I simply tell them to get the person to lie flat, to keep them warm, and help them feel safe. At some point in your life, when you or someone you know is faced with either tragic events or seemingly insurmountable circumstances follow this process to prevent the onset of shock.

Cast down imaginations

(For the weapons of our warfare are not carnal, but mighty through God to the pulling down of strong holds;) Casting down imaginations, and every high thing that exalteth itself against the knowledge of God, and bringing into captivity every thought to the obedience of Christ; And having in a readiness to revenge all disobedience, when your obedience is fulfilled. 2 Corinthians 10:4-6

The enemy wants to gain a stronghold, a position of dominance or occupation of a special place...your mind. Strongholds begin as imaginations which are mental images that are neither perceived nor present to the senses (i.e. eyes, ears, nose, and skin). Images in and of themselves are not damaging until we give place to them through meditation or prolonged mental viewing at which time negative thought pictures are extremely harmful. That is how someone can have a passing thought that there is a snake in the plumbing system waiting to swim into the tub as you take a bath have it develop into a gripping fear that can lead to serious hygienic problems. It starts as simple musing about the possibility of someone flushing a pet down the toilet, than progresses to serious rumination and actual theorizing as to how the snake could crawl through the intricate network of pipes. This is anteceded by picturing the snake's plan of attack and images of the strike right down to the very detail of when it will happen. Before you know it that person won't even set foot in the bathroom without a knife.

Obviously that is a humorous depiction; want something more true to life? Let's take a marital breakup. An acquaintance of mine was going through a divorce, and was really struggling mentally, emotionally, and as a result physically. In speaking with him I found that he had created some very serious mental images and as a result the enemy was having his way with him. My friend wouldn't eat, stopped working out, and couldn't sleep more than a few hours at a time. He was actually creating a completely new reality by the action of his thoughts and visions, and it was a bad one. You see, his former wife was a very beautiful woman who prior to the divorce had begun to plant some very negative seeds in this man's mind. After their divorce was finalized he saw himself as unlovable, and the voice of his ex rang in his ears "You'll never have anyone after I am gone. Who could ever love you?" Since that was what he continually replayed in his head he began to have actual visualizations of himself as an old man who was all alone and miserable. The truth of the matter was that he himself was good looking and could rebound, but not by wallowing in self pity and eating himself to an early grave.

The point here is the images we are capable of creating from the thoughts that pop into our heads can lead to paralyzing effects. That is why we need to take President Roosevelt's approach (see chapter introduction) and crush the snake before it actually strikes. In II Corinthians 10:5 we are given one of the most powerful weapons in the arsenal of spiritual warfare when we are instructed to cast down imaginations and every high thing that exalts itself over the knowledge of God. What this tells us is that we are just as capable of allowing our mind to create victorious effects if we free it to hear the voice of God over the din of the enemy's camp. First we have to literally "head" harmful imaginations off at the pass. I am happy to report that my compadre did just that.

Speak the Word Only

Casting down imaginations is an active defense. It doesn't happen by waiting for something magical to take place, but rather by replacing the dour images with the truth of God's word. The Bible is laced with affirmations and instructions from our Heavenly Father that are meant to keep us, to bind our wounds and set us on course to our destiny. For these promises to work for us we have to first find them which only happens when we make the knowledge of God our priority over everything else. That is what is meant by "every thing that exalteth itself". Everyday there are a myriad of things that vie for our attention, some profitable and others not so profitable, but none as valuable as the intimate knowledge of God.

My wife put it best to me. During one of the Yankees' World Series runs in the late 1990's she really wanted my attention and I was engrossed in the middle of a pivotal game. At a critical juncture in the contest, she was fuming (rightfully so) because I hadn't responded to her with anything but a passing glance. She said to me, "Go ahead and watch your game, but see if the Yankees will sleep next to you tonight." With that she walked out of the room, and, let me tell you, *that* game was no longer my top priority. It took some serious apologizing and probably a few dozen roses before I got back in Sonia's good graces. I would have done whatever it took to win her heart again.

It struck me that as cavalier as I had been with my wife on that and so many other occasions that I am ashamed to mention I have, for much of my life treated God as bad or worse. I bet if you were honest with yourself you would say the same thing. It's time we understood our sports won't save us, neither will our jobs, our favorite television shows or our fancy cars but God can and will if we will get to know Him.

Once we have that knowledge of the Word made Flesh then we need to speak the "logos" or words that are written on the pages of scripture as they relate to those imaginations. If you are dealing with mental oppression tell your mind "No, I refuse that notion that I am depressed. According to the word of God I HAVE the mind of Christ." (I Corinthians 2:16). When facing fear about your financial future, and if you are a tither you can boldly say that "No evil or plague shall come near my dwelling." (Psalms 91:10).

> IT'S TIME WE UNDERSTOOD OUR SPORTS WON'T SAVE US, NEITHER WILL OUR JOBS, OUR FAVORITE TELEVISION SHOWS OR OUR FANCY CARS BUT GOD CAN AND WILL IF WE WILL GET TO KNOW HIM.

The key is to continue to speak the "logos" (written word) until it becomes "rhema" to you. Rhema is more than just words on the page it has the connotation of God speaking to you. In other words that word is no longer a group of letters nicely arranged but is actually part of you and is living inside of you because it represents the voice of God. Find your situation in the word and cast down every thought that leads you away from the will of God in your life. Let the enemy be the one who is shocked at the words coming from your mouth.

Raise Your Core Temperature

Hypothermia is the technical term for a state in which the body's temperature cools below acceptable levels (around 98.6 degrees Fahrenheit). Since our organs and tissues require a certain amount of heat to conduct normal function even a slight drop can have extreme adverse effects. Some sources show that a one degree drop in core temperature can reduce metabolic rate by ten to twenty percent. Core heat loss significantly reduces coordination, coherence, and strength.

While in Chiropractic School my classmates and I learned a simple mnemonic, or memory phrase, to help us recall the symptoms related to hypothermia. "He's got the *umbles*" represented the fact that as hypothermia set in it was characterized by a person who mumbles, grumbles, fumbles, stumbles, and tumbles. I would say this is an adequate description for what follows when a person loses their zeal for the things of God.

As situations around us heat up, and the pressure arises it is easy to fall into the trap of mumbling, muttering under our breath about the injustices we see taking place; before you know it mumbling progresses to grumbling about leadership or even about God. "Why does God allow such evil in the world?" "Why won't He just fix my mess?" From that point it's not long before we fumble, dropping the ball that represents the responsibility we have to share the gospel and be a blessing to the nations of the world.

Once a child of God can mentally ascent to being less than what God called them to be it becomes increasingly more likely that they will stumble in their walk and open the door for sin to grab a foothold until they tumble completely out of fellowship with Daddy God.

And because iniquity shall abound, the love of many shall wax cold. Matthew 24: 12

These words of Jesus ring true today. I have heard unbelievers wanting to justify staying out of the house of God, and believers trying to excuse themselves from the commitments they have made blame the evils that are rampant in the world around them for the reason they have been hardened to the word of the Lord. It usually sounds something like this:

"Well, if God was such a loving God why would He let children get sick?"

Or this...

"How can I follow a God who allows drug dealers to live in luxury while good and honest people are getting their homes foreclosed?"

And so because of this view of the world, and the resonating shock waves they've grown cold.

Get a Blanket

I can see how someone can take this approach because

as a high school and college student I took the same view. I was angry and depressed and I blamed God for all the world's woes. I didn't verbalize it to anyone but I sure thought it. I would probably still feel that way today had a young man named Colin Lopez not been obedient to sit down with me and re-open my eyes to the *real* good news of the gospel. Jesus died for sinners.

God didn't send his son to save a bunch of goody two-shoes. He sent him to deliver people who didn't care about right or wrong, who would just as soon step on someone than to reach out a hand of assistance, who would cheat on their wives rather than honor the marriage covenant, and who wouldn't think twice about lying to save their own hides.

What kind of God would allow a child to die? The same God who allowed his innocent son to hang on a cross held up by a few nails. So now when I want to complain because my electric bill is a few dollars higher this month, or I lose a cell phone connection at a bad time, or get a flat tire on my way to work I remember that if God didn't do another thing for me, he has already done enough for me, covering my sin on that cross where Jesus hung for me.

If you ever come across a snake bite victim and they are lying on the ground shivering call for help and get a blanket under and around them as quickly as possible to elevate their core temperature. If you are snake bit the first thing you must do is stay under your covering. Don't run FROM the local church run TO it. A good church home is a place where you can be sheltered from the elements for a time, have your wounds bound up, and be nurtured back to health.

When you are under the covering of a pastor and local church who will pray for you, speak the word into your life, and give you godly advice and sound counsel your spirit will be warmed. God created the local church to be a place of refuge and refreshing. It is a community where you can receive forgiveness, restoration, lifting of burdens, and healing. I think James chapter five sums up this role of the church as a covering best:

Is any among you afflicted? let him pray. Is any merry? let him sing psalms. Is any sick among you? let him call for the elders of the church; and let them pray over him, anointing him with oil in the name of the Lord: And the prayer of faith shall save the sick, and the Lord shall raise him up; and if he have committed sins, they shall be forgiven him. Confess your faults one to another, and pray one for another, that ye may be healed. The effectual fervent prayer of a righteous man availeth much. James 5:13-16

The church is not a building, but rather a group of builders. It is men and women who are constructing the kingdom of God and fashioning kings and priest out of once beaten down people. Jesus said in John 15:11 "These things have I spoken to you... that your joy may be full."

What things did he speak? Well, for one, that we "love one another as he loved us" (verse twelve). A love like that is only forged with consistent connections. It irritates me when I hear someone write off the church or church attendance because congregations are too big or too small, too black or too white, too far away, too hypocritical and say they can get all they need by watching a televangelist and praying on their own. It's obvious they missed the point of what Jesus stated in this passage and have settled for just going to an edifice rather than being part of the move of God's Spirit that brings the body together; otherwise why would they settle for half filled joy?

Incomplete joy equals unfulfilled needs, which results in cold Christians. If you are experiencing the effects of hypothermia there is no better way to begin the warming process than getting around some fired up, imperfect but forgiven men and women, and letting the flame that is on the inside of them spark the kindling in you. Enjoy this type of fellowship inside *and* outside of the church building and before you know it the thoughts in your head will be of victory and health, the words emanating from your mouth will be life and warmth to your core and to those around you, and your actions will demonstrate that you've been touched by the Almighty.

The Spirit of God, the Master, is on me because God anointed me. He sent me to preach good news to the poor, heal the heartbroken, Announce freedom to all captives, pardon all prisoners. God sent me to announce the year of his grace— a celebration of God's destruction of our enemies— and to comfort all who mourn, To care for the needs of all who mourn in Zion, give them bouquets of roses instead of ashes, Messages of joy instead of news of doom, a praising heart instead of a languid spirit. Rename them "Oaks of Righteousness" planted by God to display his glory. They'll rebuild the old ruins, raise a new city out of the wreckage. They'll start over on the ruined cities, take the rubble left behind and make it new. You'll hire outsiders to herd your flocks and foreigners to work your fields, But you'll have the title "Priests of God," honored as ministers of our God. You'll feast on the bounty of nations, you'll bask in their glory. Because you got a double dose of trouble and more than your share of contempt, Your inheritance in the land will be doubled and your joy go on forever. Isaiah 61: 1-7 (The Message)

"IF YOU ARE GOING TO BE ALL
GOD HAS CALLED YOU TO BE, NOT
SOMEONE WHO LOOKS BACK AT ALL
THE MISSED OPPORTUNITY AND
WASTED POTENTIAL THEN YOU HAVE GOT
TO LEARN TO ENCOURAGE YOURSELF."

"A WEAPON WHICH YOU DON'T HAVE IN
YOUR HAND WON'T KILL A SNAKE"

AFRICAN PROVERB

CHAPTER 7

YOUR FIRST AID KIT, WHAT TO DO WHEN A SNAKE BITES

"The will to win is not nearly as important as the will to prepare to win."

Bobby Knight

Any person who frequents the outdoors, whether it be a rock climber, hiker, or camper knows that accidents of all sorts can and do happen. Even the most experienced outdoorsman can come across a situation that they haven't seen before or a danger that may prove to be beyond their ability to handle. When you are far removed from the comforts of civilization time can be of the essence and often time is the difference between death and life. For such instances it is absolutely essential you have at your disposal something that can mitigate the damage and potential for injuries to be even more serious.

A.J. RUBANO, D.C.

Hazak

The Giant Killer and future king of Israel, David didn't always have it so good. In fact he spent a good portion of his life hiding from, outsmarting, and trying to outrun King Saul who was on a personal vendetta to eliminate David. It was during this time that David was inspired and wrote many of the Psalms recorded in the Old Testament. He used this time of desperation to reach out to the Lord for comfort, as his source of strength and protection. He had already been anointed King, many years before by the Prophet Samuel, and yet found himself living a nomadic life with every day a struggle for survival. Now, I've felt in my life like I was struggling to survive. When as a nineteen year old I fathered my first daughter and was going through the ups and downs of a tumultuous time in the relationship with my wife all while working full time and going to school full time. I experienced the questions that one asks of one-self when going through a prolonged separation from my wife and experiencing financial hardship in a place far from my family and the support system I had grown up with. But I still cannot fully imagine what must have been going through David's head and heart at this point in his life. Always on the run, always up against the wall, a spear or bow and arrow pointed directly at him, as he longed for the fulfillment of God's promise to him. It must have seemed like an eternity away. Needless to say David knew heartache. He knew betrayal.

As a warrior he also knew victory. Isn't it like the snake, though, to try to knock you off your high point. I think he does it for two reasons. First, he wants to get you thinking in the religious mode that says God wants to keep me down so He can keep me humble. It's sad but true for many believers. Because they do not know the character of the God we serve they think hard times are a punishment for their success in any area, to keep them from getting a big head. Secondly, I believe the enemy often strikes after a high point for us is because he wants to take our eyes off of what God is capable of doing in our lives and cause us to shrink back from where we are destined to go. To the place where those who know their God go, the place of strength and great exploits. (Daniel 11:32)

Stop the Blame Game

So David knew victory, he was famous for the great victories he and his mighty men had pulled out. After one such victory it's recorded that David and his men came back to their homes only to see their entire village burned down and their wives and children taken away as prisoners. To make matters worse for David his men had now turned on him and were preparing to stone him.

(Why is it that for many of us when things go wrong in our lives the first person we look to blame is never the man in the mirror. It is shameful that members of the body of Christ are so quick to turn on their pastors, as if the men of God have control over the decisions and circumstances in our lives.)

Not a Genetic Condition

Over the last fourteen years I've noticed a disturbing trend in medicine. The diseases that are wreaking the most havoc on people are not the result of bad genetics but rather diseases of excess. Things like heart disease, liver disease, lung cancer, and Type II diabetes all can be prevented (or at least to a large extent controlled) by exercising better discipline in our lives. Using more restraint in the things we put in our mouth would go a long way in reducing the death toll related to these diseases. Perhaps even more disturbing, though, is what I hear coming out of people's mouth in relation to these and other conditions like alcoholism. For some reason, and this is especially true in the people I see who won't get better, the problem is never due to something that is *there* fault. Either it was there mother's fault because of the way she cooked while they were growing up, or their dad's fault because he was too busy working to get them more interested in sports. For others they blame their job for causing so much stress they need a few drinks to relax and they don't have the room in their schedule to exercise. With people who continually shift the responsibility for their condition to someone else I simply tell them they are welcome to continue to hold this view so long as they want to hold onto their problem.

Put Blame to Shame

David found himself in a predicament, even he had never experienced before. In the past when Saul was pursuing him he at least had the unfailing support of his mighty men. Now, even they were ready to take out their frustrations on God's anointed one. Rather than panic, what did David do? Did he cry out why me? Did he give up? No and No.

He did the only thing he knew how to do, he did what he had trained himself to do when hard times and impossible circumstances presented themselves. He hazaked himself!!

He what?

SHAKE OFF THE SNAKE

He Hazak (ed) himself. You heard right.

The motto of the boy scouts is to always be prepared. Well, in your first aid kit you need to always have a hefty supply of Hazak for the situations that catch you off guard. When the snake lunges out at you there is no guarantee your buddy or your pastor, or even your spouse is going to be around to pick you up. Who knows, maybe just like David you could find yourself all alone, with even a few judgmental eyes staring right at you, menacingly. Before you go to the nearest pharmacy looking for a big box of hazak let me stop you right there because this stuff ain't available in stores, and you can't get it for three low payments of $9.95.

Let's take a look back for a moment at David as he returned home from the battlefields.......

When David and his men came to Ziklag, they found it destroyed by fire and their wives and sons and daughters taken captive. So David and his men wept aloud until they had no strength left to weep (I Samuel 30: 3-4)

I don't know if you've ever been in a situation where you felt you couldn't even muster the strength to shed a tear. One thing I can tell you is, it is a condition I wouldn't wish on my worst enemy. When I was going through a period of separation from my wife I got to this point. It was a pain and a weakness that is almost impossible to put into words. The best way I can describe it is that it was beyond emptiness. I felt tired, beaten, limp like a blown up doll with all the air released so that only the sand at the base was anchored to the floor. I am sure what David felt, returning from battle to find his home burned and family gone would make my situation look serene by comparison.

A.J. RUBANO, D.C.

David would have been justified to complain about his predicament, to ask "why me?" But his response is a great example to anyone who is facing insurmountable odds, because he proved with the Lord on our side there is no such thing as insurmountable.

And David was greatly distressed; for the people spake of stoning him, because the soul of all the people was grieved, every man for his sons and for his daughters: <u>but David encouraged himself in the LORD his God.</u> (I Samuel 30: 6)

Turn the Tables and Recover All

Everyone around him was wrapped up in their own grief, focused on their problem on what they had lost. Instead of complaining, belly aching, or murmuring David turned the tables on the enemy and so turned the tide in his direction. He "encouraged himself in the LORD" and the Bible goes on to say he pursued, he overtook, and he recovered all. The word for encouraged in this passage is a Hebrew word pronounced HAH ZOCK. I want you to know that if you are going to be all God has called you to be, not someone who looks back at all the missed opportunity and wasted potential then you have got to learn to encourage yourself. You can't always count on your brother or sister, you can't always depend on your momma or papa. You can't expect there to be a coach to pick you up off the ground and say it is going to be alright. It's great when you have it, but one thing I notice about not only David, but other great men and women of God is they have enough of God in them that when tough times and hard situations come their way they find strength in themselves to be reminded of what God has done in the past on their behalf and what he is willing to do in the future.

God Did It Before and He Can Do It Again

Encourage yourself by mentally reviewing your past successes and what God has done for you in the past. Remember the times when He has snatched victory out of the hands of defeat. Trouble does come, but it doesn't last always. If He has come through before, he will come through again. If He has given you the skills, ability and talents to be successful in the past, those skills are still available to you for future successes. STOP replaying those negative failure thoughts and do as the word commands you to, thinking on things that are good, just, and profitable. (Philippians 4:8)

Don't stop there. David encouraged himself yes, AND he also pursued. He prayed and sought the face of the Lord and then He acted. Replay the past successes than take the action needed to get you motivated. Whether helping someone else, or taking steps to come out of your own personal, business, or relationship slump. It won't just magically happen. You've got to do something.

And the Lord said unto him [Moses], What is that in thine hand? And he said, A rod. And he said, Cast it on the ground. And he cast it on the ground, and it became a serpent; and Moses fled from before it. And the Lord said unto Moses, Put forth thine hand, and take it by the tail. And he put forth his hand and caught it and it became a rod in his hand. Exodus 4:2-4

Moses had no confidence in himself or in his ability to lead the Israelites. He was worried the people wouldn't believe him and said as much to God (see verse 1). He did

131

however have a rod in his hand and he had *El Shaddai* backing him up. Even so he still had to, in obedience, use what he had. It is not your responsibility to make things happen, but you are responsible for using what is at your disposal. No matter how small or insignificant your resources or talent may seem, with God behind it, *it's* enough.

Bust out of Your Slump

I'll never forget my own personal slump experience. Here I was a leader in the church I attended and I was going through emotional burnout. I was ready to give up, to quit my practice as a chiropractor, sell my house and move to Hershey PA to become a house parent at the Milton Hershey School. It would have been so easy. No mortgage to pay, good benefits, free chocolate, free food. But it wasn't really what God had called me to.

It was the path of least resistance, but it wasn't the path God had mapped out for me. Here I was feeling sorry for myself because things weren't going quite the way I wanted them to. I decided before making a rash decision I would speak with my pastor to get his perspective on the situation. It was during this meeting that God reminded me of an event that had taken place about a year earlier. A word he had given me that I took to heart, but failed to act on. He had instructed me to go out on my own in practice and break off the partnership I had been a part of for seven years.

It was a confirmation of something my wife had shared with me months earlier, and yet I hedged on making the jump. But now, some ten months later it finally hit me why I was experiencing this "slump". It wasn't because I was in the wrong profession or didn't have what it took to be a success. It was because I failed to act on a directive from

God. I hadn't committed a sin, in the sense of the word *most* people perceive as sin; but I ignored something that was designed for my benefit.

No wonder I was feeling defeated, no wonder I wasn't reaping the rewards that were promised me. I learned a valuable lesson that day,

You cannot expect God to keep giving you new revelation when you don't act on the revelation He has already given you.

Pray, yes. Encourage yourself, yes. And then *act* on what the Lord gives you.

Resistance from your own Flesh

One thing you have got to know when the need to Hazak yourself exists. Your flesh, your physical man is never going to want to do it. It's like I was sharing with my eight year old daughter when I first got her involved with exercising. She would complain about not wanting to do it, or how much it hurt, or how hot she was, or how much she wanted to watch Kim Possible. And then she asked me if I *wanted* to exercise.

I told her, just like I am about to tell you. Most days I do not want to go to the gym and workout, or at least my physical body doesn't. My mind does because it knows how good it feels to sweat and have a rush of endorphins go through my body and the exhilaration of accomplishment, my spirit does because it knows how I use the time to pray and close off the cares and frustrations of the world around me, but my body, most of the time would rather take a nap.

Your body is going to fight you tooth and nail because you are breaking out of the comfort zone. The good news is your will and your spirit were created to conquer the flesh.

> YOUR SPIRIT WAS CREATED
> TO CONQUER THE FLESH.

The Snake Antidote- Building up your resistance.

Not all outdoorsman keep it on them, but I would venture to guess the wisest ones wouldn't be caught without it and neither should you, *Anti-venom*. Believe it or not anti-venom is actually made up of snake venom. Much like the vaccinations used to inoculate against certain diseases snake antidotes utilize a small dosage of snake venom. The venom is typically injected into an animal so that the animal can produce antibodies against the poison which can then be used to counteract the poison when injected at its normal strength.

When the antibodies to the poison are present they provide a RESISTANCE to the action of the snake poison. The Bible tells us **"Submit yourselves therefore to God. Resist the devil and he will flee from you."** (James 4:7). Notice it doesn't say pray and he will flee, or fast and he will flee, it doesn't even say God will resist him for you and he will flee. It says for you and me to create a barrier to his vile poisons so that they cannot invade and take over our lives and the good things that God has in store for those who love HIM.

SHAKE OFF THE SNAKE

If you are going to shake off the snake in your life you must build up your resistance to discouragement. Just as you need to resist the temptation to sin, you also need to resist the temptation to be discouraged, disappointed, let down, down trodden, defeated, broken, beaten, dismayed, disillusioned, and distressed. Those things are all a state of being that God has given you the authority to dispel. The resistance to them all is already in you, because if you are a believer those snake venom antibodies have been welling up inside you since the day you became Christ's and He became yours.

"The word is nigh you, even in thy mouth, and in thy heart, that is the word of faith......" (Romans 10:8)

Listen to this my friend: *Faith filled words pouring out of your mouth, even when you don't feel faith filled, have the power to free you from the shackles of the enemy.*

> JUST AS YOU NEED TO RESIST THE TEMPTATION TO SIN, YOU ALSO NEED TO RESIST THE TEMPTATION TO BE DISCOURAGED, DISAPPOINTED, LET DOWN, DOWN TRODDEN, DEFEATED, BROKEN, BEATEN, DISMAYED, DISILLUSIONED, AND DISTRESSED.

Don't get caught with your words inside you

In my study on snakes and the effects of snake poison

one of the saddest stories I read about involved a man who was an accomplished outdoorsman and yet surprisingly had a very unique fear. This rough and tough man of the wild could face off against a grizzly bear, scale vertical cliffs, go for days eating nothing but nuts and berries, but he couldn't tolerate needles. Not surprisingly he had never been vaccinated or given any type of injection his entire adult life. He hadn't even ventured into a hospital or doctor's office for the fear that they might try to trick him into being "jucked" (that's a technical term meaning to prick the skin) with a needle. According to the story he was traveling in the Rocky Mountain region traversing wooded, rough, and rocky terrain when he stepped into a snake nest and received a seemingly harmless bite from a baby snake.

As he continued to walk, however, he soon realized this wasn't a harmless bite, but the bite of a poisonous species. He quickly radioed for help to a nearby ranger station. He did everything he knew to slow the spread of the poison, and sat down near a stream and splashed some water into his face. He was always known to be an extremely well prepared hiker and indeed kept a first aid kit with him at all times when in the woods. He even had a vile of snake anti-venom, for this particular type of snake.

That, though, is where this snake story takes a rather sad twist. When the rangers found this man his heart had already stopped beating. He lay dead with a full vile of snake anti-venom and an unopened syringe on the ground next to him, apparently too fearful to inject the one thing that could have saved him.

Here's The Point

Faith filled words POURING out of your mouth are

powerful and will produce the desired result because the Word of God cannot return void (Isaiah 55:11). But those same words bound inside of you, are like the vile of anti-venom waiting to be used but with a skin that has never been pierced through with the syringe. If you are going to shake this thing you must begin speaking, begin declaring, and begin decreeing what you want, not what you see going on around you.

A Tourniquet: Your Tool to Stop the Spread of Poison

Now watch this. Proverbs 18:21 tells us that "Death and Life are in the power of the tongue and they that love it will eat the fruit thereof" so if you are struck by a snake and need to cut off the natural flow of poison your words literally become the tourniquet. Not only that, but unlike a natural tourniquet your words can reverse the process of death and produce life into a dying or seemingly dead situation.

> FAITH FILLED WORDS POURING OUT OF YOUR MOUTH, EVEN WHEN YOU DON'T FEEL FAITH FILLED, HAVE THE POWER TO FREE YOU FROM THE SHACKLES OF THE ENEMY.

My wife and I were having a discussion about this very topic; *the power of our words*. We began to conclude amongst ourselves that no one would, in their right mind, "love" the fruit of death. Secondly we concluded that for words to really have this kind of power we have to truly believe them.

With that in mind how could anyone speak death over their own life… loving it *and* believing it? Here's how. As with anything our temperaments, personalities, and experiences play a very important role in the decisions we make, and perhaps more importantly where our self worth comes from. Think about this for a moment. You are a child of strict, perhaps even harsh, parents who never attend your school events, do not recognize your accomplishments, and may even make light of your shortcomings. BUT, when you are sick, they shower you with attention. You get the royal treatment, chicken soup, ice pack, hot tea; the whole nine yards so to speak. Your situation probably isn't identical to this, but the names have been changed to protect the innocent.

Now fast forward ahead twenty years. Look at the attention I get from my peers when I am struggling emotionally, experiencing difficulty financially or sick. I may not love being sick, I may not love the pain I feel, or the lack of financial resources I have, but boy do I love the attention. I love when the pastor comes over for a home visit, and the calls I get from the leaders of the Church. Before you know it your words start to line up with what you crave, you start to buy into it, and presto, whammo, you *are* the victim. Well today is where you say, scratch that, *shout* NOOOOOOOOOO!

Munchausen

During my training at Life University's School of Chiropractic I learned about a condition known as Munchausen Syndrome; it is a psychiatric disorder in which people will literally fake illness to draw attention to themselves. It is also known as Hospital Addiction Syndrome. In some cases to make their stories more believable these people will actually injure themselves or in a related condition called Munchausen by Proxy will induce sickness in their children. The disease can be very difficult to diagnose because the people afflicted with it become so adept at hiding, and will often go to hospitals and doctors' offices several hundred miles away to avoid detection. Seeing cases like these, even in the classroom setting, revealed to me just how powerful the desire for attention really is and how quickly someone can create the victim mind set.

Start Speaking To Your Situation

The word says we can decree a thing and it shall be established (Job 22:28). Decree that you are free indeed. Decree that you are not depressed. Decree that you are all God called you to be and moving closer to becoming the man or woman he has called you to be. Decree that you are more than a conqueror, articulate that your finances are blessed, vocalize the fact that your family is blessed, and that your body is healed. That snake will have to fall off into the fire.

Stay Calm

One thing any snake bite victim needs to understand is that despite the pain and swelling that is likely to ensue following the piercing of their skin by the snake's fangs is that they must forge ahead and maintain a calm demeanor. The problem many people in this situation face is overcoming their own panic and shock after being bitten.

The physiology or normal function of the body is altered by not just the introduction of a poison but also by the release of chemicals by our own body. In the case of a hyper-anxious (worry) state we release hormones called epinephrine which can literally speed up the flow of blood by increasing our heart rate. Think about this practically for a moment. While the release of epinephrine, also referred to as adrenalin, is helpful in what is known as the flight or fight response increasing our strength, speed, and visual acuity to help us either fend off or run away from a would-be attacker, in the case of poisoning it works just the opposite….. to our detriment. Increased blood flow will cause the poison to attack and damage essential body organs…… *quicker*.

Understanding this, can you see why we are encouraged to cast our cares upon the one who cares for us? When you are going through a trial, that is poison enough to deal with, there is no need to speed up the effect by worrying about the trial and every other little thing that could possibly go wrong.

Listen to these powerful words of Jesus recorded in Matthew 6:25:

Therefore I say unto you, Take no thought for your life, what ye shall eat, or what ye shall drink; nor yet for your body, what ye shall put on. Is not the life more than meat, and the body than raiment?

In other words, your Father is saying to you. "Hey, *I've* got it under control."

Psychologists say that they spend the large majority of their time counseling people who are obsessed, worried, and paralyzed with fear over what *may* happen to them. In over ninety percent of these cases the *actual* cause of the fear NEVER occurs in their lives and, yet, more so than any physical catastrophe is what has prevented them from enjoying life and living to the fullest potential of their capacity.

My father in the faith, David Demola, is noted for saying,

"Why pray, when you can worry?" He is, of course, being facetious. But the shame of the matter is too many believers are falling victims to this worry mentality. As if worrying about our problems and trials will somehow make them go away. God, believe it or not doesn't necessarily want us to talk to Him *about* our problems. That's right. He doesn't want you to belly ache about all the things that are going wrong in your life and all the obstacles you are up against.

Now, don't get me wrong here. The Bible is clear in saying that "He knows what we have need of before we even ask" (Matthew 6:32) but, it is also clear in the Word that you and I as believers have a certain authority given to us that enables us to overcome every obstacle we face.

For verily I say unto you, That <u>whosoever shall say unto this mountain</u>, Be thou removed, and be thou cast into the sea; and shall not doubt in his heart, but shall believe that those things which he saith shall come to pass; he shall have whatsoever he saith. (Mark 11:23)

Speak To Your Circumstances, Not About Them

Notice he doesn't say we should come and tell God about the mountain. He already knows about your needs, he is not blind to your problems, and *He does care* that you are struggling. He also wants us to grow up in faith to the point where we understand we can *tell the mountain about him* and it will go. Maybe right now you need to pile up all your bills and say *to* them "be cast into the sea, my God said he would supply all of my needs according to his riches in glory by Christ Jesus (Philippians 4:19)." If you are a tither and you say these things and don't doubt in your heart you can expect results (Malachi 3:10-11).

Someone needs to take her medical records and Doctor's reports that say that you are going to be stuck with this disease or that condition for the rest of their lives. The kind of condition where your doctor has thrown up his hands and said "honey, you are just gonna have to learn to live with it." You need to speak directly to that mountain of illness and tell it to go, "By the stripes of Jesus I was, am, and will continue to be healed" (I Peter 2:24). Realize this is your right as a covenant son or daughter of the King.

Stay Motivated

If you are not familiar with the name Rulon Gardner by now, I am sure in the very near future you will be because he is a modern day Davy Crocket. I am quite certain his life and times will be the subject of a made for T.V. movie, and I can't wait to see it for I am certain it will be a great source of inspiration.

Rulon is definitely not your ordinary, average, every day person. To start off he is an Olympic Champion. That alone is a story in itself. You see for him to become an Olympic Champion in his chosen sport of wrestling he had to beat a far more accomplished wrestler, hailing from Russia, who had the reputation of simply being *unbeatable*. His opponent Alexander Karelin had not suffered defeat once in the thirteen years prior to their match-up in 2000 Summer Olympics. Not only did Rulon beat him, he did it convincingly.

But his story doesn't end there. In fact that is only the beginning. Just two years after his Olympic victory Rulon and some friends were out snowmobiling in a remote part of Wyoming. Can you picture this well over 300 pound man speeding about over hills and under tree canopies on a little snow mobile?

Somehow, during the course of the trek Rulon was separated from his friends, who figured he must have gotten ahead of them and rode back to their camp site. As it neared night fall this Giant Olympic Wrestler still had not found his way back and was forced to face his toughest opponent yet; exposure to the elements.

The Power of Positive Thinking

The search for Rulon Gardner was a massive one as sheriff's deputies and local search and rescue teams went to work, first on the ground and then in the air. After over twenty-four hours they found Rulon, *alive*. By all accounts Rulon Gardner should have been dead. Soaking wet, out in the wilderness with no food, no shelter, and in sub-zero temperatures. Amazingly, he lost only one toe to frost bite. When asked by interviewers what he did to keep himself from succumbing to hypothermia and dying, Rulon said he pictured himself in a hot tub and kept thinking about how warm the water was as the jets massaged his body.

> TO BE SUCCESSFUL AT PURSUING THE DREAMS GOD HAS PUT INSIDE YOU AND OVERCOMING THE ATTACKS OF THIS LIFE YOU HAVE GOT TO HAVE A PURPOSE, A REASON FOR BEING, A REASON FOR DOING AND YOU HAVE GOT TO LEARN TO PUSH ASIDE EVERYTHING THAT IS AGAINST THAT.

Some may say that Rulon Gardner's story is one that proves the theory of positive thinking and I wouldn't disagree with that. But we can't ever forget who the author of positive thought is.

Take a look at what Psalms 1 says on that.

Blessed is the man that walketh not in the counsel of the ungodly, nor standeth in the way of sinners, nor sitteth in the seat of the scornful. But his delight is in the law of the LORD; and in his law doth he meditate day and night. Psalms 1: 1-2

What does it mean to meditate other than to think and mutter those thoughts to yourself? When you delight in the Word of God (aka the law) enough to meditate on it the power of those words and thoughts brings to life what you desired. Instead of withering in the face of circumstances you'll experience the refreshing of God in your life and prosper as a result. Read what it says in verse three of Psalms chapter one.

And he (the blessed man) shall be like a tree planted by the rivers of water, that bringeth forth his fruit in his season; his leaf also shall not wither; and whatsoever he doeth shall prosper.

Motives That Move You

What Rulon Gardner's story also proves is the power of staying motivated and not giving up in the face of adversity. To be successful at pursuing the dreams God has put inside you and overcoming the attacks of this life you have got to have a purpose, a reason for being, a reason for doing and you have got to learn to push aside everything that is against that. It may mean getting rid of relationships that are toxic to your dreams, it probably will entail pushing aside lifestyle habits that sap your strength and cause you to be fatigued, and it definitely will include a personal walk with the Lord.

Brethren, I count not myself to have apprehended: but this one thing I do, forgetting those things which are behind, and reaching forth unto those things which are before, I press toward the mark for the prize of the high calling of God in Christ Jesus. (Philippians 3: 13-14)

The Apostle Paul's life wasn't marked by his many friends, or the people giving him a pat on the back. It wasn't marked by the wealth he had or his esteemed position in the eyes of the religious leaders. It was, however, marked by his pursuit of God and the calling on his life. What's your high calling? Who are you pursuing? Is it a face to face fellowship with the Alpha and Omega? Is it to lead your family into a better relationship with God? Is it to be someone who is a source of strength for others? Maybe it's to get as many people into the kingdom as possible, or keep the children in the nursery happy so their parents can enjoy service. Whether it's to be a leader in business or a leader in your local church or youth group, it is and should be a source of inspiration to you to cause you to press on to your higher calling.

How Else Can I Stay Motivated

I talked briefly about getting out of toxic relationships.

Those are the ones where you feel like you need to take a bath after the conversation is done, or the ones that leave you feeling like a punching bag (both physically and literally). But, don't just get out of bad relationships, get into good ones. Who are the people who when you get around them you feel like you can conquer anything, who say things that motivate you, who make you feel good about yourself. This may need to be face to face, but it can also come from listening to speakers like your pastor. I enjoy hearing from my father in the faith, David T. Demola, my pastor John Antonucci as well as from speakers like Zig Ziglar, Tommy Tenney, and Joel Osteen. The point is with modern technology being what it is I can get the encouragement, from the Word of God, and from a voice that ignites the fire inside me twenty-four/seven.

Hurting People Hurt People, Who Are You Putting The Hurt On?

Stay motivated by putting the needs of others before you. I know it is trite, but, let's face it in this country we have things pretty easy relatively speaking. When you consider what others are going through in various parts of the world it can make our problems seem small.

The times of my life when I was hurting the most are times when I set out to do the most damage to the enemy. I think I took that expression "Hurting people hurt people" to a whole new level by sticking it right in the snakes face. If you are gonna hurt someone then by all means put the hurt on the devil.

When you are down just try telling five people what Jesus did for them. If you lead just one person to salvation I guarantee you it will feel better than the best feeling you can imagine. Pray for healing or deliverance for someone else you know who is struggling. It worked for Job:

> **IF YOU ARE GONNA HURT SOMEONE THEN BY ALL MEANS PUT THE HURT ON THE DEVIL**

And the LORD turned the captivity of Job, when he prayed for his friends: also the LORD gave Job twice as much as he had before. (Job 42:10)

God wants to liberate you from the victim mentality. Why else would he call you a *more than a conqueror*. God wants you to be a force for HIS kingdom, not a punching bag for the enemy. So don't stop with praying and believing. When you get into action you take your motivation to a whole new level. And when you get slapped in the face when you are on the offensive, when you get knocked down when you get in the enemy's face, do like my friend, the Rev. Joe Balina, says "Don't give up, GET UP!!!"

That's the life of a true believer. Believe, Pray, and Act..... get knocked down.... Get back up...... Believe, Pray, and Act again and.............

Then see God go to work...........

"IN THE SPIRITUAL ARENA THERE
IS A VERY REAL PROTECTIVE HEDGE
THAT GOD KEEPS AROUND
THOSE THAT LOVE HIM AND
ARE CALLED BY HIM.
IT IS A HEDGE THAT IS SO STRONG
IT IS ACTUALLY IMPENETRABLE,
UNLESS WE OPEN IT."

"LOOK BEFORE YOU LEAP FOR SNAKES
AMONG SWEET FLOWERS DO CREEP."

UNKNOWN

CHAPTER 8

PREVENTING THE BITE

*"The superior doctor prevents sickness; the
mediocre doctor attends to impending sickness;
the inferior doctor treats actual sickness;"*

Chinese Proverb

I n a recent children's movie entitled "Over the Hedge"
the fictional lives of a host of wildlife are followed as a
raccoon on the lamb from his loan shark attempts to
use an unsuspecting group of squirrels, turtles, and a skunk
to help him pay off his debt. The story goes on to show how
their serene life is turned upside down as they make the four
foot journey from one side of the hedge that separated their
animal kingdom to the other side ruled by humans.

They soon found out that despite the lure of free junk
food, life on their side of the hedge was not nearly as peril-
ous as it was on the human side, where trained dogs, cars,
and pest control presented a serious threat to their survival.

This hedge that provided a wall of safety to these animated characters reminds me of some historical walls
erected to be a source of security and protection for the
peoples they enclosed.

A.J. RUBANO, D.C.

Be On Guard for the Sneak Attack

In Homer's epic The Iliad we are told of the fight be-tween the Greeks and the people of Troy which waged on for nearly ten years. During the time of this violent struggle termed the Trojan War the Greeks attempted every military strategy at their disposal to penetrate the fortified city, and yet, despite their best efforts were unable to break through the wall that surrounded Troy. That is until they devised a plan to win the battle from the inside out.

Understanding the high regard in which the Trojans held horses and with a cunning knowledge of the Trojans religious practices the Greeks devised a plan to "flee" the battle scene as defeated foes and leave behind a large wooden horse which they knew would draw the attention and admiration of the Trojans and would be received as a token to appease their gods. Inside this wooden horse, however, was a battalion of brave and mighty Greek warri-ors on the ready to infiltrate the walled city of Troy.

Just as expected the Trojans received the "gift", rolling the colossal wooden horse inside the perimeters of their fortress and rejoiced in their victory. And just as planned the walls of Troy were finally penetrated and the Greek's victory soon ensued.

In this day and age we don't have much need for large concrete barriers surrounding our towns to ward off enemy invasion in the natural realm, although sometimes I really do wonder. But in the spiritual arena there is a very real protective hedge that God keeps around those that love Him and are called by Him. It is a hedge that is so strong it is actually impenetrable, unless we, like the unwitting Tro-jans, open it. In other words it can only be broken from the inside out. Often times it is the things we are most comfort-able with that enable the opening of the hedge. We become lulled to sleep and complacent and before we know it the enemy has infiltrated many of the areas of our life we thought were safe.

Then Satan answered the Lord and said, Doth Job fear God for nought? Hast not thou made an hedge about him and his house, and about all that he hath on every side? Thou has blessed the work of his hands and his substance is increased in the land. Job 1: 9-10

Are You Sabotaging Your Hedge?

Most of us look at the story of Job and see a man who was greatly afflicted, but we miss the fact that God himself placed a hedge about him and "blessed" all that he had. That hedge and that continued blessing in his life would never have ceased had the hedge not been opened.

Now let your religious mind go for just a minute. I know there are some who have taught and who actually accuse God of opening the hedge and playing games with Job's life, and justify it by using the words Job spoke when he was admonishing his wife, "The Lord giveth and the Lord taketh away." But if you inspect this passage a little more closely you will see God DID NOT open the hedge around Job. Let me direct your attention to one word; *Behold*. We don't use it much in our modern vernacular. But we do use its cousin, *Look*.

And the Lord said unto Satan, <u>Behold</u>, all that he hath *is* in thy power... Job 1: 12

In other words somewhere in the past, or in something that Job either did or felt in his heart he had created a crease or a crack in God's protective hedge around him and all that he had. While I am not precisely sure which thought or action it was I can point to a couple of attitudes that certainly would fit the bill as potential culprits. One is fear and the other is lack of unity.

He that diggeth a pit shall fall into it, and whoso breaketh an hedge, a serpent shall bite. Ecclesiastes 10:8

Job was known for his piety. He was a giver, and in fact every day gave sacrifices and offerings unto the Lord. The Bible goes on to tell us his reasoning behind the offerings. In verse five of Job chapter one we find out right up front that Job "rose up early... and offered burnt sacrifices according to the number of them all (his children): for Job said, It may be that my sons have sinned and cursed God in their hearts.."

This passage reveals something about Job. He was giving to God out of a spirit of fear; he was worried his sons were sinning against God. Maybe he was concerned they were hanging with the wrong crowd. Maybe he had been so busy doing the work of the ministry and tending to his business he hadn't poured his faith into them. But for some reason this was a very real fear he had and it dominated his thought process. I don't know about you, but I usually wake up slowly and it takes a couple of hours for me to warm up before anything can get my attention. Not so for Job, he got out of bed wondering if his kids were outside the will of God.

We have got to watch that we don't fall into ruts (pits) of religiosity, or the act of doing things out of tradition. Too often these are the things that have a form of godliness but lack the power thereof. (II Timothy 3:5) Don't do something just because someone told you, or you think it is the religious thing to do. Do it because it's right and it is pleasing God.

> ### DON'T DO SOMETHING JUST BECAUSE SOMEONE TOLD YOU, OR YOU THINK IT IS THE RELIGIOUS THING TO DO. DO IT BECAUSE IT'S RIGHT AND IT IS PLEASING TO GOD.

Play to Win, not "Not" to Lose

Let me illustrate this to you in another way. I am a big sports fan, so you will have to excuse my sports analogy here (again). But like the Frank Sinatra song says, "I've go to be me" and besides God created me this way for a reason, AND…. I know there are a few sports fans in the body of Christ beside me.

But Anyway….

In the sports world something amazing often happens when a team jumps out to a big lead, and this is true especially of timed sporting events like football and basketball. Teams with large leads, change their style of play. Instead of attacking the basket, or passing the football and playing aggressive defense, they slow down their pace and try to "prevent" the other team from making up the deficit.

There is a saying in football that the only thing a "prevent defense" (a term for a low risk sagging defense) prevents is Victory. Simply put teams that get out to big leads often lose the tenacity of a winner.

So instead of playing to win…… ..
………….. they play NOT to lose.

153

A.J. RUBANO, D.C.

O sure they go through the motions of trying to win, but the fear of losing starts to creep up into the back of their minds, and if they are not careful, or if their lead wasn't big enough they set themselves up for failure.

And that was certainly the case for Job.

Are We Together Or Not?

In just a few short chapters of the book of Job during the interaction between Job and his wife we can see a very high level of disunity in conviction and belief about who God is, what His plans are for His people, and how His people should relate to Him. While Job is declaring the goodness of God, she is trying to convince him to "curse God and die." This was more than just not seeing eye to eye on a subject it was a case of outright rebellion against the foundation of their lives.

The point or position of unity is so powerful that it supplies not just double the effectiveness, but literally provides ten times the effectiveness. So revered in heaven is the agreement of just two that they will command the attention of God in such a way that He promises the fulfillment of their desires. By contrast if there is no agreement, no unified front it is impossible for two to even walk together and that can literally turn the ceilings over your head to brass hindering your prayers from reaching the father.

Unity Means Results

This need for unity in decision making is extremely important when embarking on a treatment program with my patients. It is one of the reasons why I insist that spouses accompany our practice family members when I review their examination findings and perform their first treatment. I've found after fourteen years that when the spouse realizes how severe their loved one's condition is they are much more supportive of both the expense and the commitment associated with any long term health program. In fact I've even noticed that when the spouse is involved that patients are significantly more likely to do their prescribed exercises, attend back school classes, and are less likely to miss an appointment which means they will get the results they are looking for. Often times as a result of seeing the commitment we have to our practice family members the spouse becomes a patient as well. By contrast when the spouse is unwilling or unable to participate in my patient's care there is a much lower success rate, and very often these are the people who drop out of care before obtaining maximum improvement.

Is It In You?

Gatorade first popularized the "sports" drink to combat the fatigue and exhaustion that the extreme temperatures of Florida exuded on the University of Florida football team in the early 1970's. The reason the drink and others like it have been so successful is it replenishes vital electrolytes which are essential in the proper function of muscle.

It's interesting to note that Gatorade doesn't build big muscles and doesn't create the endurance that elite athletes need to perform at a high level. What it does do, however, is help create an internal environment that enables those same muscles to perform at the high levels they have already been trained to perform at. In other words it is very possible that an athlete with very big, well developed muscles, can and likely will succumb to harsh climate changes if the right nutrients are not present at the right time when he places a *demand* on his muscles.

Today marketing efforts by the company responsible for distributing Gatorade are targeted at athletes who want to perform their best in competition with the slogan, "is it in you?"

I can ask the same question of you when it comes to the Word of God. Because, like lost electrolytes wreak havoc on the abilities of well conditioned athletes, a lack of readily available understanding of the word and will of God, when a demand is placed on your faith muscles can be catastrophic.

Don't kid yourself into think you are a spiritual giant apart from the Word of God, because the snake is dastardly enough to have even tried to fool Jesus himself in regard to what "thus sayeth the Lord".

He attempted to dupe the last Adam the same way he did the first, and will most certainly try the same tactic on you IF you are not prepared.

Now the serpent was more subtil than any beast of the field which the LORD God had made. And he said unto the woman, *Yea, hath God said*, Ye shall not eat of every tree of the garden? (Genesis 3:1) (Italics added)

If you don't know what God has said about your situation or what His will is for your life you can easily be derailed. That was the enemy's goal for the Son of God when he tried to convince him to turn stones into bread and to bow down and worship him. I want you to look at Jesus' response and then see yourself doing the same.

But he answered and said, *It is written,* **Man shall not live by bread alone, but by every word that proceedeth out of the mouth of God.** (Matthew 4:4, italics added)

And again

Then saith Jesus unto him, Get thee hence, Satan: *for it is written*, Thou shalt worship the Lord thy God, and him only shalt thou serve. (Matthew 4:10)

Jesus knew what was *written* because it wasn't just on the pages of some scrolls it was actually in His spirit. So ask yourself is it in me? And if it's not get it in you!!

Get Close to the Fire

It's no secret that animals, and snakes are no different, are generally afraid of fire. If you are ever attacked by a wild beast in the outdoors, wave a blazing stick at them a few times and watch them do every thing in there power to get away from you and fast.

When it comes to your ability to achieve the dreams God has placed in your heart, it may be that you need to check the temperature of the atmosphere you are surrounded by. Chances are you will find that you've either fallen into or created a lukewarm or even cold environment. And....we all know what happens to the lukewarm (see Rev 3:16), those who walk in the middle of the road, straddling the line between being "sold out for Jesus" or just being a "sell out".

If you want to shake off the snake and move upward and onward to fulfilling the desires of your heart, turning up the heat on your relationship with the Lord Jesus Christ is just the prescription for you. But before you go off trying to work up an emotional high, based on the feelings of your flesh, remember this: He is Spirit and your relationship with him has to be based in the Spirit. It can't be worked up or made up, or else the test of time and the test of fire will cause it to burn up. Those who worship the Father must worship Him in Spirit and in truth. (John 4:23)

You've got to be around the fire to be protected from the attacks of the enemy. Let me rephrase that, you've got to have the fire *in and around you* to be protected from the devices that Satan brings your way.

Fire Exposes the Enemy

Paul gathered a pile of brushwood and, as he put it on the fire, <u>a viper, driven out by the heat</u>, fastened itself on his hand. Acts 28:3 (NIV)

One thing about evil, it doesn't like the light of day or the heat derived from a fire. People who do wrong don't do it out in the open they hide and walk about in the shadows hoping they are never discovered. They lurk in the bushes or under rocks not wanting to be noticed. Therein lies their power, in secrecy, in darkness. Fire exposes the enemy it flushes him out from hiding and puts *him* in the position of vulnerability. It shows the fear in his eyes and causes him to flee from your presence. In James 4:7 we are instructed to submit unto God. Submission to God causes us to be in alignment with the will of God and creates an environment that fuels passion in our heart's for the things of God. Therefore when you submit to the Father the enemy can only run away to get away from the harm the fire can do to him

The Fire Draws People to You

The other thing about fire is that it will attract others to you. Do you want increase in your business or to get more people involved in your ministry or department? Don't focus so much on the external, instead concentrate on stoking up the flame of God on the *inside* of you. I think it was John Wesley who said "get yourself on fire for God and men will come and watch you burn" and that is so true. People are attracted to real, sincere passion. With all the flim-flam artist out there today people are looking to men and women who mean what they say and say what they mean. Don't be fooled by what you see nationally with certain agendas coming to the forefront, be it the removal of prayer in schools or same sex marriages. These are not the wishes of the majority as some would have you believe, they are the result of the tenacious effort of a few, and in the absence of courageous, fire driven men to speak up for the truth their agendas have taken root. Now, though is the time to have the fire of God burning hot in us to root out, pull down, to destroy, plant, and build.

See, I have this day set thee over the nations and over the kingdoms, to root out, and to pull down, and to destroy, and to throw down, to build, and to plant. Jeremiah 1:10

You thought kowtowing to the politically correct would spark your success or that going along with the crowd would garner you enough favor to be at the top, don't believe it for a moment. If you are to be successful, if you are going to overcome frustration, discouragement, and the paralyzing effects of depression and self doubt you can only do it by speaking what you truly believe. Ask any leader in the sales industry the secret to the success of their top sellers and I guarantee they will tell you one hundred percent of the time, without fail that it is a firm belief in the product they are selling. I'm not talking about the flash in the pan people who have a good year and are gone; the people who excel and stick around are those who know that they know that their product or service works. They are the ones who can look someone straight in the eye and say "you need this; you will be lost without it. In fact, it will cost you more not to have it than it will to purchase it." That's what you need. As men and women of faith if we are to have staying power we are going to have to be moved by a firm trust that what God has told us in His word is absolute truth. Let the conviction that is on the inside of you be the kindling that keeps your fire going and burning bright enough to attract others.

Your Internal Fire Needs to be Hotter than the Circumstances

Then was Nebuchadnezzar full of fury, and the form of his visage was changed against Shadrach, Meshach, and Abednego: therefore he spake, and commanded that they should heat the furnace one seven times more than it was wont to be heated. ..... Therefore because the king's commandment was urgent, and the furnace exceeding hot, the flames of the fire slew those men that took up Shadrach, Meshach, and Abednego. ....Then Nebuchadnezzar spake, and said, Blessed be the God of Shadrach, Meshach, and Abednego, who hath sent his angel, and delivered his servants that trusted in him, and have changed the king's word, and yielded their bodies, that they might not serve nor worship any god, except their own God. Therefore I

SHAKE OFF THE SNAKE

make a decree, That every people, nation, and language,
which speak any thing amiss against the God of Shadrach,
Meshach, and Abednego, shall be cut in pieces, and their
houses shall be made a dunghill: because there is no other
*God that can deliver after this sort. Then the king **promoted***
Shadrach, Meshach, and Abednego, in the province of
Babylon. Daniel 3:22-30

I believe the reason that Shadrach, Meshach, and
Abendego did not burn was because they were hotter than
the fire. The fire is either going to burn you, as it did to the
guards responsible for binding the three Hebrew boys; burn
stuff off of you, like it does to gold being refined; or burn
in you and right along with you as it did in this case. Shadrach, Meshach, and Abendego had already chosen to serve
God no matter what. They were not deterred by the King's
decrees or the enemies that rose up against them.

The end result of their HOT faith was that the king, Nebuchadnezzar got a revelation about The ALMIGHTY
GOD and the three men GOT PROMOTED!!!!

> THE FIRE IS EITHER GOING TO BURN YOU,
> BURN STUFF OFF OF YOU, LIKE IT DOES
> TO GOLD BEING REFINED; OR BURN IN
> YOU AND RIGHT ALONG WITH YOU.

We, the church, have been claiming the heathen for our
inheritance. And we have questioned why we have to battle
fears, frustrations, anxieties, and the rest of the evils of this
world. This is why. As we come out of the fiery trial with

161

the fire on the inside of us the heathen will take notice and want the God we testify about.

Secondly.....

Your promotion does not come *from* man, but it does come *through* man. You have been trying with all your might and possibly beyond your might to the point of **Burn Out**. God has not called you to work so hard you burn out; he has called you to believe on HIM and burn up; to come up higher to where HE is. As the fire of God burns on the inside of you it will shine through to the men (and women) in positions of authority you come in contact with and they will favor YOU. That is where and when the promotion you've been struggling so hard to get will show up

Preparing Your Ground for Fire

A friend of mine had several family members living in the San Diego area during the wild fires that destroyed thousands of miles of land and displaced hundreds of thousands of people in October and November of 2007. When I asked him how his family fared he happily told me that his Uncle's house had been spared, adding that it was the purchase of a weed wacker that may have saved his home while all the others around it were destroyed. His uncle, it seemed, had weeded out all of the brush from his back yard several weeks before the fires were started so that when the fires came his way there was nothing for the flame to attach to and so it jumped past his property, pushed by hurricane force winds on to the next property and continued it's course from there destroying everything in its path.

It revealed to me this powerful principle:

> ## NO MATTER HOW CONSUMING OR FORCEFUL YOUR SPIRITUAL FIRE BURNS IT IS UP TO YOU TO KEEP THE GROUND IN THE RIGHT CONDITION FOR IT TO STAY LIT.

It is up to you to fan the flame by receiving from the Holy Spirit revelation and refreshing. You've got to protect your fire from wet blankets represented by bad relationships and negative influences in your life, the people who are trying to bring you down with them. And you are responsible for providing the kindling to feed the fire, through your worship and study of the Word.

You can expose the snake, fend off your enemy, and if need be feed on him.

Resist the Temptation to Pull Back

When situations arise in our lives that cause us pain, or arouse emotions of fear, anger, resentment, or frustration there is a natural tendency to pull back. If you have ever touched your hand to a hot stove top you know precisely what I am talking about.

This tendency is not just natural, it's instinctive. We don't need to think about it because it is ingrained in our DNA and in the natural realm its function is one hundred percent protective. Uncovered skin left on a burning stove top for even a few seconds can mean severe damage to the skin, nerve endings, ligaments, and even bone so believe me I am thankful that we have been given this reflexive ability. In the area of the soul and spirit, though, we need to train ourselves to trust God to be our source of protection. Although our upbringing, temperaments, and emotional responses tell us to pull back from adversity to safeguard ourselves following this pattern of protection can keep us from fulfilling God's plans for our lives.

In my capacity as a leader at Faith Fellowship Ministries I have seen people on track with God one moment and out of sight the next because of their unwillingness to trust God in trying situations. When they most needed to press in to the resources that were available to them in their church family they allowed their fear of the perception of others to be their excuse for staying away. Instead of going to the rock of their salvation for strength in their time of need they phase out of sight. Often it follows the pattern of first dropping participation in ministry. Either due to guilt, shame, or feelings of inadequacy they slow down or stop altogether their involvement with Sunday school, men's and or women's fellowship, home bible study, choir, or any other department that requires active involvement. From there the next stage is making attendance at regular church meetings less of a priority. Instead of being faithful and on fire at two services a week, you may see them at two services a month. Before too long key relationships with strong believers are substituted for more "loose" bonds with a different, less confrontational crowd who are willing to let them be.

Contrast that with what we see from Paul in the passage in Acts twenty-eight. While gathering sticks to help prepare the fire Paul is bitten by a viper. There is no mention that Paul even so much as flinched. He had every reason to. I am sure that bite hurt. I am certain it was an aggressive and violent move by the viper. So much so that the natives expected Paul to swell up and die right in front of them. He just left his hand there with the snake dangling over the fire.

When bitten by the snake Paul was indignant to its attempt to derail him. He had a mission and hadn't yet fulfilled it. He had already reconciled in his mind, in his heart, and in his spirit that like Jesus before him, he was going to the other side. The snake, no matter how venomous, was powerless to stop that.

This is the attitude we must make our own. The snake is not powerful, *we* are! The things we tribulate over can't do anything to us; they can't keep us from mending broken hearts, energizing an idea, or feeding a hungry soul. Those issues that frustrate us won't rule over us or box us in because the God in us will not be contained. His Spirit was endowed to be released through us.

Unlike those around him who were taken back by the viper's attack on his life Paul was undaunted. Through his life's journey in Christ he had already learned there was no victory in complaining. Long ago he made the decision to win, not whine. He had the mindset of a warrior, not a worrier, and therefore did not weary in the fight. There was no pull back in Paul and there is no pull back in you. Just hold that hand over the fire, let the enemy feel the heat from some godly influence. Keep it there just a little longer, let the flame of the Holy Spirit singe its tail and add a little shake of the wrist. Into the fire goes the enemy of your soul.

I don't care how much your natural defense mechanism wants to pull you away, resist it, and allow God to develop you in seasons of adversity and use you for His good pleasure. Stay close to the fire, remain plugged in where you've been planted and you will come out victorious.

A.J. RUBANO, D.C.

Use the Flames to Devour Your Enemy

Only rebel not ye against the LORD, neither fear ye the people of the land; for they are bread for us: their defense is departed from them, and the LORD is with us: fear them not. Numbers 14:9

Up to this point you've probably dealt with fear and doubt in such a way that you never even considered your enemies as a meal. Psalm twenty three tells us that the Lord would prepare a table for us in the *presence* of our enemies, so you may have thought your adversary was the guest of (dis)honor. Well I'm here to tell you that he isn't the guest, he is supposed to be the main course.

Several years ago I watched a movie with my son produced by Kenneth Copeland Ministries. The protagonist in the movie was a troubled teen who had been struggling with the loss of his father, who had died when a plane he piloted crashed when the son was just an early adolescent. The young man, who had periodic dreams about his dad that were both a source of inspiration and sadness, somehow became tangled up in a bank robbery. He wasn't the thief, but he ended up in the back of the bank robbers' truck as they made their escape to a desert area.

Somehow the boy escaped, with the money and intentions of turning in the robbers and the money, but as he ran away he was discovered and chased by the thieves. His only defense was to run up into the mountains to hide and wait out the villains. After several days in a cave without food or water he learned he had to live off the land if he was going to survive. In order to survive he had to face his fears head on, one of which was snakes. When presented with the opportunity he captured and killed a long snake which he proceeded to roast on a fire he forged by using his glasses to reflect the sun's rays on some leaves. The once feared snake became his sustenance in his time of need.

Let me encourage you, your trying situation is not as bad as it seems. That beast that looks like it wants to take your head off is DINNER. Is your business or family struggling? So is everyone else's. That is not doom and gloom; *that* is an OPPORTUNITY. Some would call that a perfect storm, because when the dust settles your competition will have been defeated and you didn't even have to do the work.

Keep the fire burning, shake off the snake into it, and feast on its remains.

"WHEN YOU REALIZE THAT THE ALL
POWERFUL, ALL MIGHTY GOD IS
BEHIND YOU AND HE IS EMPOWERING
YOU FOR VICTORY IT IS AMAZING
WHAT YOU CAN ACCOMPLISH."

"IF YOU SEE A SNAKE, JUST KILL IT ·
DON'T APPOINT A COMMITTEE ON
SNAKES."

ROSS PEROT

CHAPTER 9

STEP ON THE SERPENT

*"Men may rise on stepping-stones of their
dead selves to higher things."*

Alfred, Lord Tennyson

No matter how brave we may be, or attempt to be there will be times in our lives when we are afraid. It is interesting to note that something that may excite joy or exhilaration in one person can be terrifying to another. By that I don't mean sky diving or bungee jumping, although I am sure they can both be fun activities, but something like talking to a group of people can create very real feelings of terror.

I read somewhere once that public speaking is actually higher on the list of professed fears than death itself. Of course those surveyed had probably not seen the blockbuster movie, "Snakes on a Plane"; but, imagine that, people would prefer to be the one *in* the casket rather than being the one to give the eulogy. Fears, though, are meant to be overcome. In some cases we do that by plunging right in and conquering.

I recall learning to swim. I was with a group of other

children at the local YMCA and none of us were willing participants. I suppose the instructor could have taken a more "understanding" approach and explained in greater detail how we could work with the water to have greater buoyancy and described how so many others had learned before us. And…had he taken that approach, I believe some of us might still be standing their in our Speedos shivering in the brisk air of that indoor facility. Instead he had his assistant throw us in and with few exceptions we were all treading water and on our way to being good swimmers.

When Afraid of the Teeth Grab the Snake by the Tail

Yes, there are times when we need to hit our fears head on. As you may have already found out that doesn't work for every thing that concerns us; others require time and the hand of the Lord to be perfected (Psalms 138:7-8). Indeed, we will often be called to defeat our worries in stages or levels. I want you to see something from the life of Moses that demonstrates this point.

And Moses answered and said, But, behold, they will not believe me, nor hearken unto my voice: for they will say, The LORD hath not appeared unto thee. Exodus 4:1

Here we have Moses literally arguing with God about what he has been asked to do, to go speak to Pharaoh and tell him to let the children of Israel go free. The unspoken part of Moses words are shouting that he is afraid to go before Pharaoh. Not only does Moses expect that Pharaoh won't believe who sent him, but in addition he is not too confident in his speaking skills either (reference statistics on public speaking).

So what does God do? Does he excuse Moses? Does He tell him He'll find someone else? Does He give Moses an out? Listen to what happens next.

And the LORD said unto him, What is that in thine hand? And he said, A rod. And he said, Cast it on the ground. And he cast it on the ground, and it became a serpent; and Moses fled from before it. Exodus 4:2-3

God decides to paint Moses a picture. He starts by illustrating the effect of fear. How do I know this? Simply put, you don't run away from something you are NOT afraid of. The second that rod hits the ground and transforms into a serpent we see Moses high tail it out of there. Think about this for a moment. If the rod suddenly became a bunny rabbit, would Moses have split so quickly. We have often been taught that the rod in Moses hand represented his ability, or our abilities, and how in the hand of God they can produce great results. I don't disagree with that. In addition to that, and perhaps even more so, it may as well represent the fears we keep hidden and what those hidden fears are keeping us from.

And the LORD said unto Moses, Put forth thine hand, and take it by the tail. And he put forth his hand, and caught it, and it became a rod in his hand: That they may believe that the LORD God of their fathers, the God of Abraham, the God of Isaac, and the God of Jacob, hath appeared unto thee. Exodus 4:4-5

Notice the Lord did not tell Moses to grab the snake by the head. Perhaps he knew Moses would balk at that suggestion. Maybe He thought it better to take things one step at a time. Whatever the reason it was definitely the least confrontational route for Moses to grab the snake by its tail.

You may need to move one level at a time to overcome your adversaries. There is nothing wrong with exercising a little tact. If need be start at the tail. Grab the serpent by the tail, defeat your fears or enemies one step at a time and allow God to make your weaknesses strengths in His hands. Be like Moses. He was afraid; afraid of speaking before the people, afraid of what the Egyptians might do to him but he surrendered to the will of God.

A Win Win Situation

The Apostle Paul said "for me to live is Christ and to die is gain." When we surrender our will to the will of God the sting of death is blunted. What the Apostle Paul is talking about is a Win/Win situation. So let the enemy bring on his devices, let him form his weapons. I already know from the truth of God's word that No weapon that is formed against me will prosper, it just can't thwart me. When you can go into a battle with this mindset, the thought process that says give me your best shot devil "It might knock me down but it won't keep me down". When you realize that the all powerful, all mighty God is behind you and he is empowering you for victory it is amazing what you can accomplish.

Safe or Sorry?

This is the mindset that Joshua and Caleb had when they spied out the Promised Land on the other side of Jordan. In contrast, all the other members of their reconnaissance team came back with the report that the land was indeed flowing with milk and honey, BUT, the enemies on the other side are really BIG. These spies saw the prize God had waiting for them, knew the promises that God had covenanted with them, but were so focused on the size of the obstacle in their way that they shrunk back from pursuing God's best. The Bible says that they "saw themselves" as "grasshoppers in their own eyes". Grasshoppers are snake food. What should have been an opportunity for advancement proved to be a stumbling block. These faithless Israelites cost themselves *and* their families what they had coveted for forty years, super abundance. Their play it safe thinking robbed them of God's best for their lives, just like it can rob you and me of God's best for our lives *if* we let it. We all would do well to learn from the example of David.

David was everything but conservative. He never saw a lion he couldn't tackle. There wasn't any opposing army he thought could take his mighty men. This is the thought process that David went in with when confronted with the Giant, Goliath.

Long before he was "King David", David was living like a King. By that I don't mean he was staying in posh surroundings or being taken care of hand and foot. He was still working as a Shepard yet he knew who he was in God, he understood what it meant to be the son of the King of Kings. Perhaps, that's why he is called a man after God's own heart. While all the older more accomplished warriors were unwilling to go one on one with the eight foot Philistine David welcomed the challenge. He saw Goliath's bravado and heinous trash talking as an insult to the one true God. When you and I are faced with the "hissing" of the enemy in our lives, the whispers that God can't lift us out of our predicament, the brash insinuation that our problems are not important to Him we have got to see it as an insult

173

against God himself.

David knew he had victory before he ever stepped on the battlefield. Why else would he refuse Saul's suit of armor? He recognized that there was much more at stake than just a fight against one large Philistine attacker, this was about covenant, this was about the honor of his God. I imagine he said within himself "if God is God he can handle this all on his own and I just need to be a willing vessel." One of the amazing things about David in this was the strength of his conviction. We often say "Me and God" make up the majority, but how often do we go seeking a friend or minister to "be in agreement" with us before taking a step we "know" God told us to take. All around him was negativity, his brothers were calling him cocky, his King really had no confidence in him, and I can only wonder what the rest of the battalion thought of this brash and inexperienced shepherd boy. David was unfazed. "You're going to go after that giant with a sling shot? Are you nuts?" "What if you miss David? Then what." "He's so big, if you miss him he will eat you for breakfast." David turned a deaf ear to all the nay-sayers. When they were thinking about the possibility of what ifs and planning his funeral, all David could think was, "he's so big how *can* I miss him."

And Eliab his eldest brother heard when he spake unto the men; and Eliab's anger was kindled against David, and he said, Why camest thou down hither? and with whom hast thou left those few sheep in the wilderness? I know thy pride, and the naughtiness of thine heart; for thou art come down that thou mightest see the battle. And David said, What have I now done? Is there not a cause?......And David said to Saul, Let no man's heart fail because of him (Goliath); thy servant

will go and fight with this Philistine...Thy servant slew both the lion and the bear, and this uncircumcised Philistine shall be as one of them.... I Samuel 17: 28-36

A Tale of Two Brothers

David's optimistic outlook was a trait I am sure endeared him to God. It reminds me of a story I once heard Reverend John Hagee tell about twin brothers. One was always looking at the bad side of things, an eternal pessimist; while the other could see only the good in things. The parents of the two boys were concerned that they weren't growing up balanced so they consulted a therapist who advised that they separate the two boys into secluded rooms when it was time to celebrate their birthdays. He told them to give the pessimistic son nothing but the best presents. He added that to the optimist they should only give a box of manure.

When the birthday rolled around the parents did exactly as they had been instructed than peeked in on the two boys as they opened their gifts. The pessimist hurriedly unwrapped all of his presents, a computer, video games, a remote control car, and a dvd player. He was heard saying "what an ugly color for this computer, I bet this car doesn't even have any batteries, this dvd player will probably break." The optimistic son, on the other hand, lifted the lid off the unwrapped box of manure and began to laugh as he tossed it in the air, "you can't trick me, where there is this much stuff, there has got to be a pony!!!"

I believe David grabbed five stones, not because he thought he might miss, but, because he wanted to be prepared to take out the rest of Goliath's brothers.

A.J. RUBANO, D.C.

To The Victor Goes The Spoils

(There are eleven days' journey from Horeb by the way of mount Seir unto Kadeshbarnea.) And it came to pass in the fortieth year, in the eleventh month, on the first day of the month, that Moses spake unto the children of Israel, according unto all that the LORD had given him in commandment unto them; Deuteronomy 1: 2-3

We are often told in Faith circles that without a *test* there is no *test*imony. But being tested in and of itself has no guarantee of reward. It is only when we *pass* the test, when we overcome the obstacles that are placed around us or go to the next level in our decision making do we become eligible for the spoils. The Israelites had what should have been an eleven day "pop-quiz". A short trip from where they crossed the Red Sea to the place they were expected to cross the Jordan. Forty years later they were still moaning, still complaining, still not believing in the God that miraculously delivered them from the hands of their oppressors. Each time they would get close, someone else in the camp would begin to talk bad about their leader, "I tell you, that Moses he needs to get his head examined, we were better off before we met him. I could be twice the leader he is." After dropping back, they'd make up some ground until someone else piped in "I'll just take a little extra manna this time, no one will notice." Little issues, small foxes, *disastrous consequences*. Ultimately that group never did make it. God had let them die off and than allowed the next generation, and Joshua and Caleb to cross over.

The Israelites plight was not unlike a friend of mine (who shall remain nameless to protect the innocent). We spent the better part of three and a half years together going to school to obtain our doctorate degrees in Chiropractic. During that time he relied heavily on me to help him get through core classes like biology, anatomy, physiology, as well as many other technical subjects related to our field. Even though he was an excellent technician when it came to our craft of spinal adjusting, with my help he still struggled, but at least managed to pass these technical core classes. He was and still is a really nice guy, but someone I might accurately describe as a little lazy. Looking back I may have done him a disservice by helping him as much as I did, because he constantly justified his lack of study in these technical areas by saying he wouldn't really use those lessons in actual practice. It was a statement with some validity, but beside the point nevertheless. His attitude, though seemingly harmless based on his ability to pass examinations at our school, came back to haunt him when he took the National Board Examination for the first time and promptly failed the two technical sections, *badly*. While certainly this was costly from the standpoint of having to re-take the exam which at the time was about six hundred dollars per section, even more costly was the fact that it would keep him from sitting for his state board for an additional year and missing out on an associate position in a prominent practice in Boca Raton. At an expected salary of about one-hundred thousand dollars per year this was a big loss.

If We Don't Learn From Our Mistakes
We Are Bound To Repeat Them

You would think that losing one hundred thousand in salary, spending an additional twelve hundred dollars for exams and spending an additional year in limbo would have been motivation enough for my friend to realize the value of actually studying. He didn't. In fact he endured two more failing efforts of the National Exam, following this same methodology of belittling the importance of the technical sections, before finally getting to sit for his State Exams. Again lack of preparation proved to be his downfall, as it took him two and a half years before finally passing this set of exams on the fifth try. He literally cost himself well over a half million dollars in income and his parents' sanity all because he wouldn't discipline himself to pass the test so he could proceed to the next level.

A Step Up

David's victory over Goliath put him in line for positional and financial reward. King Saul promised his daughter's hand in marriage and a share in the successes of the kingdom. But more importantly, because he didn't wait to act on God's word, his disciplined obedience and willingness to stand up for God solidified his standing with the The Almighty. He had already been anointed king, but had now taken a kingly step in his development.

I like what David did when faced with the challenge of Goliath. He didn't play with his adversary, he went right after him, and after he struck the fatal blow he didn't walk away without finishing the job. He slew the giant and then cut off his head to make sure there was no chance for his return. Too often we, rather than take the proactive approach of slaying our adversaries allow them to hang around. The man with a weakness for pornography is crazy to keep open access to internet porn sites and check out the *Sports Illustrated* swimsuit issue, the woman who wants to lose 20 pounds is kidding herself if she thinks she will accomplish her goal with bags of chips in her pantry and gallons of ice cream in her fridge, the couple that wants to get out of the financial rut is deluded if they believe they can open up another credit card account and pay down their debt. No wonder the frustration mounts and you feel like you are at the proverbial end of your rope.

You have got to literally and forcibly remove the adversary from your premises. If need be get rid of your television, put a lock on your ice-box, and cut up those credit cards and when the snake attacks, don't see it as the end of the line, look upon it as the beginning of your coronation. Look at it as a vital cog in your advancement to fulfilling your divine destiny and purpose.

And I will put enmity between thee and the woman, and between thy seed and her seed; it shall bruise thy head, and thou shalt bruise his heel. Genesis 3:15

As you place your foot on the neck of the enemy, crushing the life supply of both the internal and external snakes in your life, it will be a springboard to greater and better things for you and the people in your sphere of influence. Unlike the world system which uses people to climb up the corporate ladder, kingdom advancement uses the strongholds of the enemy to further serve and lift up others. Whereas the modis operandi of this age is to win for me, God's system calls for us to overcome, receive the blessing, and be a distributor of that blessing.

Not only does God *want* you to overcome the snake's plan for you, it is His highest and best for you that you do so. Just like David you've got to know He can handle it on His own so long as you are a willing vessel.

No *Ill* Effects

But Paul shook the snake off into the fire and suffered <u>no ill effects</u>. Acts 28:5 (NIV)

The author of the book of Acts was clear in stating that Paul was not hurt by the viper that grabbed hold of him. There were no ill effects. A further study of the passage revealed though that there most certainly were positive consequences of the event.

The people expected him to swell up or suddenly fall dead, but <u>after waiting a long time and seeing nothing unusual happen to him, they changed their minds and said he was a god</u>. There was an estate nearby that belonged to Publius, the chief official of the island. He welcomed us to his home and for three days entertained us hospitably. His father was sick in bed, suffering from fever and dysentery. Paul went in to see him and, after prayer, placed his hands on him and healed him. Acts 28: 6-8

Initially the islanders that witnessed this snake attack perceived it as an indication of Paul's guilt. Only a guilty man could survive a shipwreck only to be poisoned by a snake and die hours later, was the thought that ran through the camp. They saw it as retribution from a judgmental God, as often is the case today.

When we experience the loss of a loved one or unfortunate circumstances in our own lives for some reason many people see it as something God has done to us. Even young children tend to believe this, and who could blame them after they have been told by their parents, aunts, and uncles that the reason a loved one died was because God needed another flower for his garden. I know it sounds good, but it's not true. God is not responsible for the problems in your life, He doesn't give us love tokens of cancer (Exodus 15:26 "the Lord that healeth thee"), he doesn't make us poor so that we can be humble (Deuteronomy 8:18 "the Lord thy God....that giveth thee the power to get wealth"), and the Bible is clear in telling us that he doesn't tempt us either.

While God is not the author of temptations and the efforts to kill, steal, or destroy your life (John 10:10) he will use the tactics of the enemy to help fulfill His overall plan for our lives and to help *us* see what lies in our hearts.

After watching Paul shake off the snake into the fire, you'll see a different perspective from the inhabitants of the island. Now, they looked upon him with awe and respect. They said among themselves "he is a god". They attributed to him supernatural powers. As a result of their reverence for Paul they called upon him to heal the father of the head honcho on the island. Paul was given an open door.

Before you let your religious mind go tilt, asking why Paul allowed the natives to call him a god, consider that Paul used this platform not to glorify himself, but to give honor and glory to Almighty God. He had the attention of the men that shared his company, and now had the favor of a top official.

Think about that. How often in our churches and in our individual lives have we sought after, worked for, and attempted to conjure up key or strategic relationships. Maybe months or years have gone by with these efforts failing to pan out the way we'd hope for. In just a matter of days Paul had all of this.

Talk about a plan blowing up in the enemy's face! Not only had he failed to take out Paul, he had literally set him up to bring salvation to the people of Malta and receive the monetary means to continue his journey.

When this had happened, the rest of the sick on the island came and were cured. They honored us in many ways and when we were ready to sail, they furnished us with the supplies we needed. Acts 28:9-10

What do you think the people around you are going to say and do when they see you handle the adversity in your life, God's way, and come out the other side on top? They will want to know, who is this God you serve and how can I get to know him.

More importantly what can you expect to see transpire in your relationship with God as your "snake" experience reveals to you the status of your heart? God doesn't need to see you go through a trial to determine what is in your heart. He already knows what you have need of (Matthew 6:32). Though the inimical efforts of the snake are meant to derail your drive to fulfill the ultimate purpose for your life, if handled correctly they will unwittingly play a key role in your life's course by helping you find out what you are made of; showing you the areas you need more work on as well as what you've progressed to mastery in. Ask yourself, would David have been as well prepared to battle Goliath had he not already conquered the lion and the bear? Would his life have had the impact on others if he just sailed along from the sheep herd to the throne of Israel?

More Then Just Words

I shared with you earlier about a time in my life when I was separated from my wife and children for an extended period due to some challenges in selling our business. During that time period my grandmother, who years earlier had been told she only had days to live only to be healed by the power of God, declined in health and passed away. As it turned out the fact that I was able to stay in New Jersey for a few extra months gave me the opportunity to spend some quality time talking with her and visiting with her. We had a special bond, I had been privileged to share my faith with her when she was on her "death bed" years before and I recall as I spoke over her that "she would not die but declare the works of the Lord" that she had such a sparkle and faith in her eyes. She had a child's heart. I knew that God had ordained that time for me and Grandma Flo.

What has stuck in my head, as it relates to this passage of scripture, happened on the day of my grandmother's funeral. After a lovely memorial service and the internment at the cemetery our family got together at a nearby restaurant. My uncle, my brother, and I were in the men's restroom of all places when my brother took me aside and said that he had taken notice of how I handled myself during this period of separation from my family and how much it touched him and had given him a respect for me and for what God was doing in our lives; my uncle seconded his thought.

For years I had shared the *words* of the gospel with both my uncles and brother, but it was the action of overcoming the adversity sent my way that ministered to them the life of The Word.

Failure Is Not Fatal

After seeing what David did to Goliath at such a young age you might be tempted to say "I guess my time has passed me by…" Let me stop you right there because noth-

> "DEVELOP SUCCESS FROM FAILURES.
> DISCOURAGEMENT AND FAILURE ARE
> TWO OF THE SUREST STEPPING STONES
> TO SUCCESS." DALE CARNEGIE

ing could be further from the truth. Even if you have failed in the same area repeatedly I can guarantee you God is not finished with you yet, and he has not written you off. That being said, when failure looms in your past you need to rise up and develop a sanctified initiative, also know as guts.

Each time you get closer to the point you failed at the previous time the more likely it is for your mind to go into overdrive and run the clip of your personal movie. But just as your brain can role footage of failure it can also help visualize victory.

Role the Video, Please

Let me give you an example that is close to home. I am an avid golfer. One of my favorite things to do on a Saturday morning is to play a round of golf with my pastor and good friend John Antonucci. I think Pastor John and I like playing with each other for several reasons. First it's the godly company, we can always share our challenges and visions for the future knowing that we can trust what we share won't find its way to the gossip column. Second is the understanding that when it comes to trusting God and following Him we are on the same spiritual page. And third, we both are competing against ourselves to put up our best score each time.

One of the things Pastor and I have learned together is that golf is as much, if not more so, a mental game than a physical game. Why else could we go out and score really well one day and just one week later look like we had never played the game before. Perhaps one of the things that revealed to me the mental aspect of the game is the uncanny tendency to hit great shots over and over again on the same holes and by the same token hit poor shots over and over again on others. A case in point is the seventh hole on our home course.

If You Don't Like what's Playing Change the Reel

Let me tell you first of all I do not believe in luck. As you probably are well aware the number seven, in the vernacular of the world system, is the number most closely associated with good luck. This seventh hole for me was anything but. No matter what club I would choose to play or how well I struck the golf ball on this hole something bad would ALWAYS happen. It was as if my golf game morphed into rookie status the second I stepped onto that Seventh Tee. After having played close to sixty rounds of golf on this course I was yet to par the seventh hole. Every other hole (thirty five of the thirty six holes on two courses) I had pared multiple times, but for some reason not number seven. One day I realized that my thought process was what was getting in the way of success on this hole, so the last time I played it I did just what I am telling you. When I stood up to hit the ball the same negative thoughts began to flood my mind as had the previous fifty nine, but this time instead of taking back the club I backed off, rebuked the thought that was in my mind and replayed the Good Success I have experienced on so many other golf swings. The result, a beautiful drive placed right in the middle of the fairway followed by two other well struck perfectly placed golf shots and two putts for my first par EVER on number seven.

Had the hole changed, was I suddenly a better golfer. No and No. I simply stepped back from the failure and reviewed what I was capable of. Failure is not fatal. Missing the mark is not wrong, it is just human.

Brethren, I count not myself to have apprehended: but this one thing I do, forgetting those things which are behind, and reaching forth unto those things which are before, I press toward the mark for the prize of the high calling of God in Christ Jesus. Philippians 3:13-14

FAILURE IS NOT FATAL. MISSING THE MARK IS NOT WRONG, IT IS JUST HUMAN.

As Mr. Carnegie said, failures and disappointments can be some of the greatest stepping stones to success. Thomas Edison can vouch for that, on his way to developing the light bulb he learned (approximately) nine thousand-nine hundred-ninety-nine ways how not to. If you ever do any home maintenance you are probably familiar with a product that no handy man should be without, WD-40. It is not called WD-40 because it has forty different patents or forty different chemicals in the mixture. Water Displacement fortieth attempt is the result of thirty nine other attempts that didn't go quite as planned. In 1941,the year Ted Williams of the Boston Red Sox became the last man to hit over .400 (.406 to be precise) a feat that hasn't been repeated in over sixty years he had a total of one hundred eighty-six hits, and by contrast made two hundred seventy outs. Perhaps one of the greatest tales of using past failures to spur great success was none other than our sixteenth president. Abraham Lincoln considered by many to be our greatest president lost at least eight attempts at election to various political posts, and failed miserably as both a businessman and a farmer. Failure is never final and it is never fatal unless *you* say so.

What are you Going to do with your Past Failures?

I shared with you earlier about a classmate who had difficulty convincing himself that he needed to study for a certain part of his board examinations and as a result cost himself about four years of his life taking and retaking expensive examinations. It would be easy to say he was a loser, and based on the effect of those failures on his psyche it would have been easy for him to just give up and find a new career path. I am happy to say he didn't take that route. He finally decided to listen to sound advice, got a tutor, put in the hard work and passed the exam. He now has a successful practice and has helped a lot of people fulfill their dreams of good health. The key is he had the final say and he never said quit.

> FAILURE IS NEVER FINAL AND IS NEVER FATAL UNLESS YOU SAY IT IS!

A.J. RUBANO, D.C.

You Musn't Quit

When things go wrong, as they sometimes will,
When the road you're trudging seems all uphill,
When the funds are low and the debts are high
And you want to smile, but you have to sigh,
When care is pressing you down a bit,
Rest! if you must - but never quit.
Life is queer, with its twists and turns, As every one of us
sometimes learns,
And many a failure turns about
When he might have won if he'd stuck it out;
Stick to your task, thought he pace seems slow-
You may succeed with one more blow.
Success is failure turned inside out-
The silver tint of the clouds of doubt -
And you never can tell how close you are,
It may be near when it seems afar;
So stick to the fight when you're hardest hit
It's when things seem worst that you musn't quit.

Author Unknown

SHAKE OFF THE SNAKE

When the Invitation to Quit Comes, Decline It.

I'd be lying if I told you that from the time I gave my life to Jesus until now it has been all smooth sailing; *far from it*. There have been times when I felt I don't have the strength to fight and others when I felt like giving up. I've known the emotion of feeling I've let people down, let myself down, and let God down. And I have been tempted on many occasions to simply throw in the towel. It is at times like this I feel like Satan owns stock in Fedex and he sends via special, overnight, priority delivery an invitation signed and sealed and meant for every man or woman of God who has ever walked the face of the earth. It is an invitation to give up the fight, to turn tail and run.

When that invitation makes its way to your door do yourself and everyone that knows you and everyone that needs to know you and be touched by you a favor. Take a big, black sharpie the kind T.O. (Dallas Cowboys football star Terrell Owens) used to sign that infamous football (you sports fans know what I am talking about), and mark in bold, legible print.....

RETURN TO SENDER

Each and every time you are presented with the opportunity to quit, refuse it like you refused lima beans when you were a kid. Send it back, and like Emeril Ligassi, the famous television chef, turn up the heat in your life a whole 'nother notch.

"WHEN YOU KNOW WHAT THE
ENEMY IS GOING TO ASK BEFORE
HE ASKS IT, AND EVEN MORE
IMPORTANTLY WHEN YOU KNOW
HOW YOU WILL ANSWER BEFORE
YOU ARE PRESENTED WITH THE
CHALLENGE YOU HAVE A
DECIDED ADVANTAGE."

"UNLESS YOU KNOW WHAT
YOU'RE DOING, THERE
IS NO SAFE WAY TO
HANDLE A SNAKE, NONE."

MATT PRICE

CHAPTER 10

THE REAL SECRET TO SNAKE CHARMING

"The beating on the tail of the snake may stop his progress a little, but the more vital parts must be struck before his poisonous death-dealing venom will be wiped out."

George Washington Carver

O n city streets in India where the practice of snake charming, as we now know it, likely originated it is apparent that this mystical form of entertainment is becoming a lost art. Due to the proliferation of cable television and documentaries exposing some of the once held myths about serpents as well as laws promulgated by the Indian government restricting its use more and more snake charmers are finding new avenues of employment.

There was a time when men who hypnotized snakes were highly thought of in the region. They were noble men, typically well educated, and often served as healers using their knowledge of snakes and snake handling to treat bite victims; as well as perform pest control for citizens who wanted serpents removed from their homes.

Over the years their craft evolved into that of magicians and entertainers who were thought of as a novelty to draw tourist to the area and promote the Indian culture as performers in overseas culture fests. Today some snake charmers still provide a valuable service for the treatment of bite victims by obtaining venom for use in antivenins.

Prepare Like a Snake Charmer Should

While the "act" of snake charming appears to be dangerous the real risk occurs *before* the show begins. In many instances the expert snake charmer extracts the snake's venom gland, sews the serpent's mouth shut or defangs the reptile, often a krait or cobra. In other words, the snake charmer actually removes the viper's instrument of harm. In order to further reduce the potential for injury the charmer sits out of striking range.

There is a parallel that can be drawn between this ancient skill and our present day confrontations against the enemy of our souls.

Simply put, Prepare.

My friend, Pastor Joseph Fortunato, said something to me once that has stuck in my mind and something that has had a significant impact on me both personally and professionally.

It is more important to be a private success than a public success.

What that has meant to me over the years is that before I expect to receive anything I need to get and stay right with God. Before I can stand in front of the congregation and declare what God's word is saying for their lives I've got to apply that word to my own life. Prior to telling my patients what is best for them I need to incorporate those same health secrets into my program. Standing and waving my arms in worship before the sanctuary is great so long as I commit to spending time alone with my Lord Jesus. Otherwise everything I do is merely a pretense.

Defang the Snake

As an expert in soft tissue injuries I am often called upon to testify or give my medical opinion for a case that has legal implications. While I am not a lawyer I have found that thinking like one has helped me be of better service to the people I care for as their attorney presents the facts pertinent to their file.

Since the medico-legal arena is an intrinsically adversarial one it is important that I anticipate the questions the opposing counsel may pose. In every instance my client's rights, potentially large monetary compensation, and my reputation are at stake.

One of the best strategies I have found to take the teeth out of the defenses efforts to discredit my expertise or minimize the relationship between the accident and my patient's injuries is to address any possibly questionable issues early on in the questioning *by the plaintiff's attorney* (the plaintiff is the person who was injured and is making a claim or law suit). It is especially important that I demonstrate a precise knowledge of my patient's medical history and activity status before their accident occurred so that I can better illustrate the effect the new trauma has had on their life.

I can tell you that I rather enjoy frustrating the defense

lawyers that depose me by stealing their thunder!

Am I a genius for developing this plan for dealing with confrontation? No, just a disciple of our advocate with the Father, Jesus.

When Jesus faced off with Lucifer in the desert He used this exact tactic to stifle the attempts to distract Him from completing the steps that were necessary to fulfilling the destiny His Father had mapped out for Him. Recall the showdown recorded in Matthew chapter 4 and pay attention to the number of times Jesus declares "It Is written."

Then was Jesus led up of the Spirit into the wilderness to be tempted of the devil. And when he had fasted forty days and forty nights, he was afterward an hungered. And when the tempter came to him, he said, If thou be the Son of God, command that these stones be made bread. But he answered and said, <u>It is written</u>, Man shall not live by bread alone, but by every word that proceedeth out of the mouth of God. Then the devil taketh him up into the holy city, and setteth him on a pinnacle of the temple, And saith unto him, If thou be the Son of God, cast thyself down: for <u>it is written</u>, He shall give his angels charge concerning thee: and in their hands they shall bear thee up, lest at any time thou dash thy foot against a stone. Jesus said unto him, <u>It is written again</u>, Thou shalt not tempt the Lord thy God. Again, the devil taketh him up into an exceeding high mountain, and sheweth him all the kingdoms of the world, and the glory of them; And saith unto him, All these things will I give thee, if thou wilt fall down and worship me. Then saith Jesus unto him, Get thee hence, Satan: for <u>it is written</u>, Thou shalt worship the Lord thy God, and him only shalt thou serve. Then the devil leaveth him, and, behold, angels came and ministered

unto him. Matthew 15: 1-11

When you know what the enemy is going to ask before he asks it, and even more importantly when you know how you will answer before you are presented with the challenge you have a decided advantage. It is like going into a final exam after having already seen the answer key.

By knowing what is written and fully understanding what God has *already* said about the outcome of your circumstances you can readily disarm the adversary and walk in victory.

One caution, though. No snake is going to just open his mouth and let a snake charmer yank his teeth out. The serpent will do whatever it can to wriggle out of the charmer's clutches. It may flail its tail or make some other violent move in an effort to twist out of captivity.

The devil is no different. Based on his dialogue with Jesus we can see that he knows the Word and knows how to twist the meaning of the Word to his liking.

It takes diligent study of the Word to discern that shade of perversion on the enemy's lips. The reason Jesus knew what was "written" was because he applied himself to search the scriptures. You can do the same. Today we have at our disposal a litany of resources to help us gain insight and understanding of the Bible. There is available to you everything from Bible schools and Christian Universities to a multitude of online devotionals, study materials, and classes. Use them to defang your enemy and catapult you to the breakthrough life you know God has for you.

Lull the Enemy to Sleep

The visual picture that first comes to mind when one

thinks about an Indian Snake Charmer is that of a man wearing a turban, sitting with his legs crossed on a straw mat, and playing a flute while rhythmically gyrating his arms and upper torso.

It is interesting to note that it is this rhythmic motion, and not the music that actually hypnotizes the Cobra. Believe it or not the same affect can be realized by simply waving a straight stick in front of the snake in a similar fashion.

For some reason the shape and motion of the object have a way of captivating the serpent and lulling it into a trance like state. That is powerful and has spiritual implications.

Want to grab your adversary's attention and at the same time still him in your presence?

Develop a lifestyle of worship and praise God with all your heart. I know it sounds cliché, but there really is power in the praises of God's People. Your worship reaches the Father and sets in motion all of heaven to go to work on your behalf.

O LORD, our Lord, how majestic is your name in all the earth! You have set your glory above the heavens. From the lips of children and infants you have ordained praise because of your enemies, to silence the foe and the avenger. Psalm 8: 1-2 (NIV)

The King James Version translates that word "praise" as "strength". I find that interesting. The strongest people I have met in my life are not the ones with the biggest muscles or the most bravado. Believe me I've known some pretty huge and physically strong men that have collapsed under the weights the world has dropped on their shoulders.

No, the mightiest men and women I know, the ones

who I would want standing in a ditch with me and the first people I would call in a time of crisis are those believers who know how to worship and praise God from the very core of their being.

Up until now you may have thought praise was a fast song and worship was a slow one. Maybe you believed it was found in a specific dance, or a loud shout amongst a group of people. While those are all aspects of praise and worship allow me to persuade you that real worship is much more than that.

Jesus saith unto her, Woman, believe me, the hour cometh, when ye shall neither in this mountain, nor yet at Jerusalem, worship the Father. Ye worship ye know not what: we know what we worship: for salvation is of the Jews. But the hour cometh, and now is, when the true worshippers shall worship the Father in spirit and in truth: for the Father seeketh such to worship him. God is a Spirit: and they that worship him must worship him in spirit and in truth. John 4: 21-24

When Jesus encountered the woman at the well in Samaria after reading her mail and telling her "everything she had ever done" he explained to her that God isn't found in a specific city (Jerusalem) or church (this mountain) and the Father is looking for people who wouldn't just pay him lip service or try to cover up their apathy with fluff, but would worship Him in sprit and in truth.

It is sad for me to say but when I look around the church I see a lot of people who come on Sunday just so they can say that they were there and feel good about not sleeping in to midday. While the music is being played they are looking out in space, maybe they clap a little or even try to sing a few notes but they never really enter into God's presence. So it is obvious to me that praise and worship are not found in a song.

As the snake charmer is able to halt the normal activity of a King Cobra simply by waving a branch so you can lift up effectual praise to the King of Kings without even opening your mouth.

Lift Up Your Hands *After* You've Lifted Up Your Heart

Perhaps you have heard the saying "Your actions are so loud I can't hear a word you are saying." Let me tell you this. You can clap your hands harder, sing louder, and dance more passionately than anyone else in the church and still not enter into worship. I have known lead singers, talented musicians, church administrators, and even worship leaders who have fallen because they failed to realize that worship doesn't begin with well played and sung choruses, but with the heart.

> YOU CAN LIFT UP EFFECTUAL PRAISE TO GOD WITHOUT EVEN OPENING UP YOUR MOUTH

I love the praise and worship service at my home church, Faith Fellowship Ministries in Fort Myers, Florida. We have been blessed with an anointed worship leader, a true psalmist whose original songs have blessed my life immensely. What I appreciate most about Daniel Pena is that when he leads us he isn't performing, he is pouring. I believe he is able to lead us into God's presence because that is where he stays all week long, not just on Sundays. The anthem that he penned several years ago is a good description of what real praise and worship is.

The title of the song is "No Matter What." As a congregation we often make this confession, based on his song. *"No matter what I'm going to praise Him. No matter what the world may say, no matter what may come my way. I am going to praise Him, NO MATTER WHAT!"*

Imperfect People: God's Perfect Choice for Worship

God gets the glory when you tell your co-workers about him and esteem all the wonderful things He has done on your behalf. That is praise. It is a sweet smelling savor to the Father when you choose to forgive someone who hurts you. It is an act of worship when, away from the world and the noise, you speak to the Lord as you would speak to a friend and bless him because of who He is. When you defer your decisions to his wisdom and lay down your agenda that honors your Daddy.

And yes, when you make a joyful noise and sing and shout unto Him, or dance before Him without caring about what anyone might think. When you lift up your hands and magnify the Lord with a wave offering and give him a place in your heart that is reserved just for Him that *is* praise and that *is* worship. The kind our Father seeks.

Praise and worship sets us apart in Abba's eyes; and when you are privileged with that kind of favor you don't have to be perfect. David was called a man after God's own heart, not because he was sinless but because he was a worshipper. Abraham and Moses, the only two men referred to in scripture as "the friends" of God were far from faultless and still garnered the Lord's blessing because they made worship their habitation. They didn't have to be told or chided to honor God with their substance. True worship can never be legislated.

Isaac followed in his father Abraham's footsteps, lying to an enemy king about his relationship with his wife. He told the king, Rebekah was his sister because he feared the monarch would steal her and have him killed. Not only did Isaac escape the king's wrath, he was escorted out of the land wealthy and with a proclamation from the ruler himself that no one should harm him. (Genesis 26:7-11) What was the secret to this favor? Isaac was a worshiper.
Listen to what Isaac did after the king's decree.

Then Isaac sowed in that land, and received in the same year an hundredfold: and the LORD blessed him. Genesis 26:12

Its true Isaac had learned some bad habits from his dad. I am sure his fib about Rebekah wasn't his first lie; and don't get me wrong I am not recommending a lifestyle of falsehoods and fabrications, but Isaac learned something far more important from his earthly dad. He learned how to worship God. You had better believe this was not the first time he had planted a faith seed. "That Land" referred to in this passage was Gerar. At the time of Isaac's sowing Gerar was in a severe famine. So harsh that many people had left and headed for refuge in Egypt. In obedience to Jehovah, Isaac stayed.

I am convinced the reason he was able to stay and sow in drought was because he had seen Abraham live by his giving. Don't forget Isaac was there when Abraham was instructed by God to sacrifice his first born. *He was* the sacrifice.

I can imagine Isaac and Abraham sitting around a camp

fire and the patriarch sharing the story of how he gave a tithe to Melchizidek, the type and shadow of Jesus' kingly priesthood, and shortly thereafter Isaac was conceived in his one-hundred year old mother's once dead womb. Isaac was bred to be a worshipper.

Start Your Own Worshipping Gene Pool

Maybe you were not born to a family of worshippers. Heck, maybe you can say, like Rev. Jesse Duplantis when asked about his background before he became an evangelical minister, "Sinner." Perhaps you have been brought up in an environment of apathy or wickedness.

If that's the case then Praise God, *you* get to be the standard starter in your family line of sainthood. In fact one of the most powerful leaders recorded in the Bible can make a similar claim. I want you to see how his bold lifestyle of praise and worship helped him and the people of Israel shake off the snake that had dogged so many of the leaders that had gone before him.

It came to pass after this also, that the children of Moab, and the children of Ammon, and with them other beside the Ammonites, came against Jehoshaphat to battle. *Then there came some that told Jehoshaphat, saying, There cometh a great multitude against thee* **from beyond the sea on this side Syria; and, behold, they be in Hazazontamar, which is Engedi. And** *Jehoshaphat feared, and set himself to seek the LORD, and proclaimed a fast* **throughout all Judah. And Judah gathered themselves together, to ask help of the LORD: even out of all the cities of Judah they came to seek the LORD. And** *Jehoshaphat stood* **in the congregation of Judah and Je-**

rusalem, in the house of the LORD, before the new
court, *And said, O LORD God of our fathers, art not thou
God in heaven? and rulest not thou over all the kingdoms
of the heathen? and in thine hand is there not power and
might, so that none is able to withstand thee? Art not thou
our God, who didst drive out the inhabitants of this land
before thy people Israel, and gavest it to the seed of Abraham thy friend for ever? And they dwelt therein, and have
built thee a sanctuary therein for thy name, saying, If,
when evil cometh upon us, as the sword, judgment, or
pestilence, or famine, we stand before this house, and in
thy presence, (for thy name is in this house,) and cry unto
thee in our affliction, then thou wilt hear and help.* II
Chronicles 2: 1-10

When faced with a multitude of enemies the first thing
Jehosaphat did was pull out all the *spiritual* stops. He
didn't call for all the archers, nor proclaim a draft for all
men over the age of eighteen. He implored the people to
join him in acts of praise and worship; fasting, praying,
seeking the Lord's face, and remembering the miracles God
had wrought in Israel's past. They magnified the name of
the Most High God; but it didn't stop there.

O our God, wilt thou not judge them? *for we have no
might against this great company that cometh against us;
neither know we what to do: but our eyes are upon
thee........*Then upon Jahaziel the son of Zechariah, the
son of Benaiah, the son of Jeiel, the son of Mattaniah, a
Levite of the sons of Asaph, came the Spirit of the
LORD in the midst of the congregation; And he said,
Hearken ye, all Judah, and ye inhabitants of Jerusalem,
and thou king Jehoshaphat, *Thus saith the LORD unto
you, Be not afraid nor dismayed by reason of this great
multitude; for the battle is not yours, but God's.* II

SHAKE OFF THE SNAKE

Chronicles 20: 12-15

In response to their unified cry, under the direction of Jehosaphat, the Lord God responded by pouring his Spirit upon Jahaziel and pronouncing the victory he had in store for his people; even providing them with a pre-game analysis of how the battle would go down.

Ye shall not need to fight in this battle: set yourselves, stand ye still, and see the salvation of the LORD with you, **O Judah and Jerusalem: fear not, nor be dismayed; to morrow go out against them: for the LORD will be with you.** *And Jehoshaphat bowed his head with his face to the ground: and all Judah and the inhabitants of Jerusalem fell before the LORD, worshipping the LORD.* **And the Levites, of the children of the Kohathites, and of the children of the Korhites, stood up to praise the LORD God of Israel with a loud voice on high. And they rose early in the morning, and went forth into the wilderness of Tekoa: and** *as they went forth, Jehoshaphat stood and said, Hear me, O Judah, and ye inhabitants of Jerusalem; Believe in the LORD your God, so shall ye be established; believe his prophets, so shall ye prosper.* **And <u>when he had consulted with the people, he appointed singers unto the LORD, and that should praise the beauty of holiness, as they went out before the army, and to say, Praise the LORD; for his mercy endureth for ever.</u> II Chronicles 20:17- 21**

Let me set the stage here. God tells the children of Israel that this battle won't require them to get their hands dirty. He asks only for them to believe in Him, and in doing so he promised that the battle was His. Jehosaphat then leads the people in a worship service to beat all worship services and establishes a front line marked, not by infantry men but, by a parade of singers praising the Lord. I can imagine this was one powerful passionate choir and because they sought God with all of their heart the victory over their enemy was assured.

And when they began to sing and to praise, the LORD set ambushments against the children of Ammon, Moab, and mount Seir, which were come against Judah; and they were smitten. **For the children of Ammon and Moab stood up against the inhabitants of mount Seir, utterly to slay and destroy them: and when they had made an end of the inhabitants of Seir, every one helped to destroy another.** *And when Judah came toward the watch tower in the wilderness, they looked unto the multitude, and, behold, they were dead bodies fallen to the earth, and none escaped.* **And when Jehoshaphat and his people came to take away the spoil of them,** *they found among them in abundance both riches with the dead bodies, and precious jewels, which they stripped off for themselves, more than they could carry away: and they were three days in gathering of the spoil, it was so much.* **II Chronicles 2:22-25**

Think about it. It took *three* days to gather all the gold, silver, precious gemstones. Talk about an upgrade in lifestyle. Jehovah Gireh, the Lord your provider is more than willing to help you shake off the snake and increase you when you put him at the center of all that you do and become a true worshipper.

Jehosaphat was a flawed man. During his reign he established several unholy alliances. Like his father, Asa, he failed to remove the high places of pagan worship in Judah. Despite these shortcomings his life and in particular his leadership in responding to the invasion of the Moabites, Ammonites, and Edomites demonstrates the dynamic ca-

SHAKE OFF THE SNAKE

pacity inherent in our praise and worship.

Make God your habitation. Honor him with your actions and melodies will flow from your heart. Even if you can't hold a note you will be an instrument for his glory; a flute that will still your enemy, and one more skilled than any Indian snake charmer.

Position Yourself above the Snake

Another crucial element to the snake charmer's success is the posture he places himself in prior to beginning his performance. Once the charmer and his assistants find a suitable location for their show they place a mat on the ground and the charmer sits cross-legged approximately three quarters of his snake's length away prior to playing and waving his *pungi* (also known as a been), the flute like instrument fashioned from a gourd.

There is a very strategic purpose for this specific way of sitting. According to those in the know a Cobra is incapable of striking objects above their head. By maintaining a position above the snake's head the risk of an attack is greatly reduced. No wonder some snake charmers will go so far as to kiss the cobra on the top of its hood (the flap of skin behind a Cobra's head).

The Bible says the same thing about the enemy of our soul in declaring "greater is he that is in us then he that is in the world" (I John 4:4). The devil is not going to make an overt strike when you are positioned properly in relation to Jesus. Oh, he may poke his head around a little, slithering to the left and to the right looking for an opening, but as long as you are hovering above the fray and over his hood his power is neutralized.

Jesus emphasized this power positioning throughout his

ministry. As the snake charmer trains his apprentices and teaches them by example our Lord modeled a life of prayer demonstrating that victory is best pursued while prostrate.

> THE DEVIL IS NOT GOING TO MAKE AN OVERT STRIKE WHEN YOU ARE POSITIONED PROPERLY IN RELATION TO JESUS.......
> AS LONG AS YOU ARE HOVERING ABOVE THE FRAY AND OVER HIS HOOD HIS POWER IS NEUTRALIZED.

We have often been taught that "leaders are readers", given my druthers I much prefer a leader who is connected to God daily through a strong prayer life. While reading can provide us with insight and information only communication with God through the dialogue of prayer will bring true impartation.

As an elder at Faith Fellowship I am regularly called upon to encourage the members of our church in the area of giving. As somewhat of a control freak I like to have everything worked out as to what I will share before I leave my house in the morning because I want to leave a legacy of excellence. One thing I began doing shortly after being given this assignment by my pastor John Antonucci was to ask God before every service to give me the words to speak that would bless the people and cause them to excel in their giving so that God is free to pour out His blessings on them.

After three years of teaching on the tithe and offering I continue to get fresh revelation from God. I have learned that the message I have prepared is subject to change at His moments notice, and he always backs up the word He gives me either through the preaching of my pastor, through a prophetic word, or through the testimony of any number of congregants who have come up to me following a service to say how much the teaching meant to them or the good news of events that followed their obedience to the things I shared weeks earlier.

In the position he has placed me in God has taught me that diligence in prayer is more important than all the other aspects of my preparation. Jesus certainly thought it was.

Ask, and it shall be given you; seek, and ye shall find; knock, and it shall be opened unto you Matthew 7:7

In the original Greek text this passage actually states ask and keep on asking. Seek and keep on seeking. Knock and keep on knocking. Just because you haven't seen the breakthrough doesn't mean God isn't listening; more likely than not He is gauging *your* level of persistence. Who knows, maybe you need a deeper appreciation for what it is you are asking for; whatever the reason keep on asking, seeking, and knocking.

I shared with you earlier about the fact that my wife and I experienced a time of separation before God supernaturally healed our relationship. One of the things I believe led to our break up was the fact that I had taken her and our relationship for granted. I was so focused on getting my education I didn't see that I was harming her emotionally by putting her dreams on the back burner and internalizing the stresses and pressures I was under without getting her involved in the process.

> JUST BECAUSE YOU HAVEN'T SEEN THE
> BREAKTHROUGH DOESN'T MEAN GOD ISN'T
> LISTENING; MORE LIKELY THAN NOT HE IS
> GAUGING YOUR LEVEL OF PERSISTENCE.

After praying and believing for four years you better believe I won't take Sonia for granted again. I don't know if that would be the case if God had simply restored our family in the snap of His fingers. Though I didn't understand it at the time He was building something in me. He was molding me on His wheel to be a vessel that could bring comfort to other men and women and building some toughness in areas that were too vulnerable. Without a doubt Daddy knew what He was doing in fashioning our marriage to stand the test of trials and challenges that were yet ahead. I thank him for allowing me to come boldly to his throne of grace every day and for the strength I received while alone with Him in my prayer closet.

Prayers that Stop the Enemy in his Tracks

Since moving to Florida I have seen my share of snakes slithering across roadways, driveways, in flower beds and even on the golf greens while I've putted. For the most part, with the exceptions of some ornery water moccasins, these creatures want less to do with us than we do with them.

On one occasion my wife was horrified to see a large black snake squirming its way through the St Augustine grass in our backyard, pausing every few feet to pop its head up for a gander at its surroundings. When it eventually slithered up to a space just outside our rear window and in front of the entry way to our lanai it prompted a frantic telephone call and some shrieks about a "killer" snake crawling up our down spout (only a *slight* exaggeration).

When I returned home, being the brave husband that I am I boldly strode to the rear of our property, golf club in hand, to further assess the situation. After a few minutes of intense investigation I was able to assure Sonia that the snake had left the grounds and was definitely not in the down spout.

She wondered how I was able to determine this, especially given my aversion to snakes as a whole. Somewhat proudly I pointed to the "tracks" that were visible in the mulch along side our home and explained that based on this evidence it was obvious the snake had mobilized in a direction away from the down spout most likely fearing the return of the master of that domain, me.

All kidding aside, if praise is considered the weapon of choice for "stilling" the avenger than prayer is what sends him packing and moving out of your zip code. Was I to record every incident where God miraculously delivered one of His servants after they earnestly sought Him in prayer there wouldn't be enough annals to contain every breakthrough, healing, or deliverance. Some were offered in public settings, while others were private. Intercession was made with long flowing poetry while cries for assistance may have been the utterance of a single passionate word, "Help!!!" The common denominator in every one was the belief that God is who He says He is and that His promises are true, regardless of what anybody else has to say. You don't have to be a seasoned veteran or orator to pray effectively. In fact age and experience have nothing to do with it.

Paul made that clear in his writings telling us in James 5:16 (AMP) that "the earnest (heartfelt, continued) prayer of a righteous man makes tremendous power available [dynamic in its working]." The only qualification is righteousness. If you are a Christian that condition was met when you accepted Jesus as your Lord and Savior.

After seeing how God moved in the life of Josiah I am certain he can do the same for you and me.

Josiah, we are told, began his reign as king at the age of eight after his father Amon was killed by his own servants. Amon had "done evil in the sight of Lord", and according to the testimony in II Chronicles 33:22-23 "sacrificed unto all the (pagan) carved images" and "humbled not himself before the Lord."

Having grown up in this type of household Josiah certainly had every excuse not to follow after the Lord. Instead he chose to walk in the ways of his ancestor, King David. At the age of sixteen, the eighth year of his kingship, he decided to get serious with God.

For in the eighth year of his reign, <u>while he was yet young, he began to seek after the God of David his father</u>: and in the twelfth year he began to purge Judah and Jerusalem from the high places, and the groves, and the carved images, and the molten images. II Chronicles 34:3

At age sixteen I was too busy thinking about what I was going to wear to impress the girls at my high school and what I was going to do to get my parents to allow me to attend a co-ed party. Not so for the young king. Josiah was so bold as to tear down the places of pagan worship and rid Israel and Judah of the priests of iniquity. Such was his zealousness to purge the city that it is recorded in verse seven of II Chronicles thirty four that he "had beaten the graven images (of foreign gods) *into powder*" (italics added).

When he had completed the purification of the kingdom he then went about repairing the house of the Lord. God rewarded him greatly for his obedience, just as he has promised to bless us when we decide to tear down the old waste places of sin and disobedience in our life and repair the temple so it is fit to be inhabited by the Holy Ghost (I Corinthians 6:19).

The gift of God to Josiah was recovery of the lost Book of the Law. As a result of the wickedness that pre-ceded Josiah, the words of the law was not found in the hearts of the people and the written scrolls themselves had been mis-placed. When Josiah located the Book and returned it to the priest of God it saddened him greatly and he tore his clothes in disgust.

Josiah didn't stop there. He humbled himself before the Lord and desiring to lead a people who would "do all that is written in the book", inquired of the Lord for wisdom needed to restore Israel.

I want you to see what the Lord's response to the young ruler was.

Because <u>thine heart was tender</u>, and <u>thou didst humble thyself before God</u>, when thou heardest his words against this place, and against the inhabitants thereof, and <u>humbledst thyself before me, and didst rend thy clothes, and weep before me</u>; I have even heard thee also, saith the LORD. Behold, I will gather thee to thy fathers, and thou shalt be gathered to thy grave in peace, neither shall thine eyes see all the evil that I will bring upon this place, and upon the inhabitants of the same. II Chronicles 34: 27-28

Josiah's humility came up before God and he was spared the wrath that God was prepared to dole out on those who had so irreverently disregarded His commandments. His prayer consisted of heart felt crying as he lay face down trembling in the audience of the King, and because of his attitude (*not his words*) he got the answer he wanted to hear.

In Humility there is Honor

If my people, which are called by my name, shall humble themselves, and pray, and seek my face, and turn from their wicked ways; then will I hear from heaven, and will forgive their sin, and will heal their land. II Chronicles 7:14

Somewhere along the line Josiah learned what we need to commit to heart. The posture of prayer is the posture of power. In humility there is honor, there is healing, and there is deliverance from the hand of the enemy.

Learn from the Master

Every expert snake charmer, I found out, is accompanied by a team of assistants or apprentices. It seems this is the way the practice is passed on from one generation to the next, through observation of the practices and techniques of those who have mastered the art. Of course, as followers of Jesus there is no question as to who warrants the title of Master.

As apprentices of the King of Kings it would behoove us to follow the disciplines of the one who demonstrated in both word and power mastery over Satan himself. To do

otherwise would violate the law of the disciple found in
Matthew 10:24.

**The disciple is not above his master,
nor the servant above his lord.**

By all accounts Jesus was a man of prayer. He exhorted
the twelve that were with him to pray always and not faint
(Luke 18:1). He challenged those who desecrated the Temple (Matthew 21:13, Mark 11:17, and Luke 19:46). He recognized that the strength of intercession was not to be
found in eloquence of speech, even chastising the religious
leaders of his day who for "a pretence" made long prayers
yet devoured the needy widows (Matthew 23:14).

Ultimately the strength and sustenance of Jesus' life
here on Earth depended on the connection He maintained
with the Father through his prayer life.

In the motion picture "The Passion of the Christ", direc-
tor Mel Gibson captured the essence of this correlation. As
Jesus knelt to pray at the Mount of Olives, before he was to
be betrayed by Judas Iscariot and captured by the Roman
Guards, the camera tracked the path of a hissing serpent as
it stalked the savior, inching its way toward Him.

As drops of blood dripped from Jesus' brow revealing
the very real toll the ordeal had taken on the son of Man
and the intensity with which He sought the Father we see
the snake suddenly shift and turn away obviously hindered
by forces unknown to the natural man. A study of the gos-
pels gives us some insight into what actually transpired.

**And he came out, and went, as he was wont, to the
mount of Olives; and his disciples also followed him.
And when he was at the place, he said unto them, Pray
that ye enter not into temptation. And he was with-**

drawn from them about a stone's cast, and kneeled down, and prayed, Saying, Father, if thou be willing, remove this cup from me: nevertheless not my will, but thine, be done. **And there appeared an angel unto him from heaven, strengthening him.** Matthew 22:39-43

At the most critical points in his earthly walk Jesus got into the stance that he found brought Him comfort, relief, revelation, wisdom, and strength. As the events leading up to his crucifixion reached a crescendo he continued in prayer and fainted not.

Follow in his knee prints, and do the same.

"THAT IS WHAT WE NEED TO DO
WHEN WE ARE FACED WITH A
KICK TO OUR MIDSECTION.
IN THE DAY OF ADVERSITY
RISE UP AGAINST YOUR CRITICS,
DUST YOURSELF OFF AND GO
RIGHT BACK TO DIGGING."

"A SNAKE DESERVES NO PITY"

YIDDISH PROVERB

CHAPTER 11

DIG A PIT FOR THE PIT VIPER

*When one door closes another one opens: but we so
often look so long and so regretfully upon the closed
door that we do not see the ones which open for us.*

Alexander Graham Bell

Then Isaac sowed in that land, and received in the same year an hundredfold: and the LORD blessed him. And the man waxed great, and went forward, and grew until he became very great: For he had possession of flocks, and possession of herds, and great store of servants: and the Philistines envied him. For all the wells which his father's servants had digged in the days of Abraham his father, the Philistines had stopped them, and filled them with earth. **Genesis 26:12-15**

As you have probably already found out there are times when the issues we face in our own lives are not our doing, or even the result of an oversight on our part. Even after standing in faith and conquering the snakes in our lives the enemy can still rear its ugly head. That is exactly what Isaac experienced at this point in his life. He faced a severe famine in his land, and while everyone around him was falling on their faces fearing the worst he did something unheard of, he sowed. I am sure his neighbors had a field day with that one. "Hey Isaac, what do you think you are doing out there beating that rock hard ground with a pick ax, working you famished oxen to the bone to plant some old, decrepit seed into the ground when there is no water in sight?"

In the United States we don't know a thing about famine. We get upset if we can't water our lawn for a couple of days, or if we can't wash our car to keep up the appearance we want. Real drought conditions, to us, are a totally foreign concept. But here is Isaac, Abraham's son, following in his dad's footsteps and planting seed at a time where everyone else was "eating" their seed. And the end result is he reaps a "hundred fold" return. I know that had to put him on cloud nine. If it was me I'd probably seriously consider the best way to rub it in the faces of all the nay-sayers.

Reign on the Parade

Unfortunately, Isaac didn't have time to do that. Immediately after harvesting his crops the jealousy of those around him came out in full force. The locals, upset with Isaac's success in the face of their struggles, stopped up the family's wells. Isn't that just like the enemy?

Imagine all the work it took for Isaac and his crew to find a water supply and dig a well, who knows how many feet deep. It was not uncommon for well depths in that region to be more than two-hundred feet below the surface before striking water. They had no back hoes or cranes to do the digging. *All* the labor had to be performed by one-hundred percent man power. This well would have been the source of water for his family, all his livestock, and his agricultural venture. Having it stopped up suddenly is a kin to the disaster a family business would face if it was burned down. Sure it can be rebuilt, but so much is lost in good will and revenue during the time it takes to repair and rebuild. That is the situation Isaac found himself in.

What does he do?

And Isaac departed thence, and pitched his tent in the valley of Gerar, and dwelt there. <u>And Isaac digged again the wells of water,</u> which they had digged in the days of Abraham his father; for the Philistines had stopped them after the death of Abraham: and he called their names after the names by which his father had called them. And Isaac's servants digged in the valley, and found there a well of springing water. And the herdmen of Gerar did strive with Isaac's herdmen, saying, The water is ours: and he called the name of the well Esek; because they strove with him. Genesis 26:17-20

He went right back to digging the wells again. There is no account of him cursing God, or asking "why me?" There is no evidence that his insurance company picked up the tab, or he received assistance from some wealthy philanthropist or friend. Isaac settled himself and his family in Gerar and went right back to digging.

It would have been easy for him to act like he had a silver spoon complex. He had already achieved great success and riches, and now he had to start all over again, *digging*. That is what we need to do when we are faced with a kick to our midsection. In the day of adversity rise up against your critics, dust yourself off and go right back to digging.

A.J. RUBANO, D.C.

Keep Digging

And they digged another well, and strove for that also: and he called the name of it Sitnah. And he removed from thence, and digged another well; and for that they strove not: and he called the name of it Rehoboth; and he said, For now the LORD hath made room for us, and we shall be fruitful in the land. And he went up from thence to Beersheba. Genesis 26:21-23

Sometimes, you are going to have to pick yourself up more than once. So what, you lost your home due to foreclosure, pick yourself up and dig, rent an apartment for a time and rebuild your credit. Saw a business go down the drain too? Find some other gameful employment for a time and ask God for the wisdom to start a new one or to rebuild your business, and better. Ask Him to show you where you went wrong and how to fix it. Take the attitude Isaac took, when his wells were stopped he didn't. He pursued that which God already had in store for him, he spoke the Word declaring "I know God said I am going to be fruitful in the land", and he received the promise.

When tough times of frustration, opposition, and attacks of the enemy come your way are you going to let the enemy dig your grave and push you in it? Or, will you be the one who keeps digging? And as you dig your way out of the mess in obedience to God's word you are digging the final resting place for the snakes in your life.

SHAKE OFF THE SNAKE

Who's Your Daddy?

> TAKE THE ATTITUDE ISAAC TOOK, WHEN
> HIS WELLS WERE STOPPED *HE* DIDN'T.

And the LORD appeared unto him the same night, and said, I am the God of Abraham thy father: fear not, for I am with thee, and will bless thee, and multiply thy seed for my servant Abraham's sake. And he builded an altar there, and called upon the name of the LORD, and pitched his tent there: and there Isaac's servants digged a well. Genesis 26:24-25

Isaac did one other thing we twenty-first century believers need to be reminded of. He remembered that his success was because of his daddy. No, not Abraham but Daddy God. Isaac dug, and dug again and when his place was settled the night did not pass before he had an encounter with God and built an altar to the LORD.

Herein lays the secret to success in "Shaking off the Snake". It is having a one to one relationship with your Daddy in Heaven. It is being so intimate with Him that the problems around you pale in comparison to His presence in your life. It comes from hearing His voice so He can direct over, through, and around the attacks of the enemy. He tells us in His word if we know Him we will be strong and do great exploits (Daniel 11:32).

In shaking off the attacks of the enemy we are free to perform the works that Jesus did and greater. (John 14:12)

In the day that you prosper remember your Daddy and

221

build an altar to him. That altar doesn't need to be a physical altar made of wood or stone; it doesn't have to be at the front of your church building. It needs to be at the forefront of your heart. Time each day to come before Him and tell Him what he means to you, why you are glad to serve him, how much more you want of Him to be revealed to you.

"WE CAN DO GOOD DEED UPON GOOD DEED, PERFORM MIRACLES, SIGNS, AND WONDERS, AND PUT UP A GOOD FRONT; BUT WITHOUT THE REVELATION OF THE ALMIGHTY ON THE INSIDE OF US IT IS ALL STRAW AND WILL NEVER GRAB THE HEART OF OUR HEAVENLY FATHER."

"METHOD IS MORE IMPORTANT THAN STRENGTH, WHEN YOU WISH TO CONTROL YOUR ENEMIES. BY DROPPING GOLDEN BEADS NEAR A SNAKE, A CROW ONCE MANAGED TO HAVE A PASSER-BY KILL THE SNAKE FOR THE BEADS."

HENRY WADSWORTH LONGFELLOW

CHAPTER 12

BURY YOUR ADVERSARY
(.....AND FOR GOOD MEASURE
STOMP ON HIS GRAVE)

*"Private victories precede public victories.
You can't invert that process any more than you
can harvest a crop before you plant it."*

Stephen R. Covey

And the LORD said unto Moses, Make thee a fiery serpent, and set it upon a pole: and it shall come to pass, that every one that is bitten, when he looketh upon it, shall live. Numbers 21:8

It seems that our God takes a special pleasure in turning the tables on the enemy. The enemy funnels attacks into our lives to steal, kill, and destroy us and God uses them for our good, at times as a way to catapult us right into our divine destiny. The enemy does his best to make us think we are weak, poor, sick, and defeated but God said he would use the "foolish things of this world to confound the wise"

(I Corinthians 1:27) and calls us strong in him and the power of His might (Ephesians 6:10), abundantly blessed beyond measure (John 10:10), completely whole (I Peter 2:24), and more than conquerors (Romans 8:37).

Remember this, Satan is a perverter. He takes what God has created and counterfeits it for his own purposes. In fact he has never had an original idea in his existence. Take music, God invented music and Satan was his "Minister of Music" before he was booted out of heaven. Music was meant to be praise and worship God. Now, look around and you see music is used in this world to glorify self, desire, sexual immorality, and even death.

How about sex? God created that too as a way for a husband and wife to come together so that the two would be made one (Genesis 2:24). Today sexual sin runs rampant, both in and out of the church with recent studies showing nearly half of men and women in the church have a problem with pornography, either in print form, on the internet, or through the television.

Believe me, though, when I say none of this has caught God by surprise. And though it hasn't caught Him by surprise I know it breaks His heart to see so many of his children so far from the level they should be at. To say it displeases Him would be a gross understatement. We can do good deed upon good deed, perform miracles, signs, and wonders, and put up a good front; but without the revelation of the Almighty on the inside of us it is all straw and will never grab the heart of our heavenly father.

It's what you do in your private times, when no one is watching, when it is just you and God that prepares you internally to succeed in the outside world. Otherwise you are building on a faulty foundation. A life built on accomplishments and deeds without the character to go along with it is hollow at best and usually leads to a big fall (reference the covers of Time and People Magazine on any given week for examples).

When You Are Falling Cry Out

The Israelites were willing to substitute the real God and the real promises of God for the counterfeit "blessings" of Egypt. They pleaded with Moses and blamed him for taking them to the wilderness to die. Many of them got their "wish" as an infestation of fiery serpents came and bit the people. Some, though, remembered the God of forgiveness and mercy and repented of their sin and cried out to HIM.

And the LORD sent fiery serpents among the people, and they bit the people; and much people of Israel died. <u>Therefore the people came to Moses, and said, We have sinned, for we have spoken against the LORD, and against thee; pray unto the LORD, that he take away the serpents from us.</u> Numbers 21:6-7

Whenever men and women have screwed up, God has always had a plan for redemption. The only thing that prolongs the agony for us is our failure to recognize our wrong and our need for deliverance. Once the Children of Israel cried out for help it was there. Moses prayed, God gave Moses the plan, Moses carried it out, and the people that *obeyed* were saved.

And Moses prayed for the people. And the LORD said unto Moses, Make thee a fiery serpent, and set it upon a pole: and it shall come to pass, that every one that is bitten, when he looketh upon it, shall live. Numbers 21:8

That's all He asks of us today. Look and Live. Instead of looking upon a serpent, though, we have the son of God. Look to Jesus, NOW, and Live.

And the law is not of faith: but, The man that doeth them shall live in them. <u>Christ hath redeemed us from the curse of the law, being made a curse for us: for it is written, Cursed is every one that hangeth on a tree:</u> That the blessing of Abraham might come on the Gentiles through Jesus Christ; that we might receive the promise of the Spirit through faith. Galatians 3: 12-14

The raised serpent in the wilderness was a type of savior, foreshadowing the work of Jesus on the cross. It was Jesus, who hung from the pole at Golgotha for all to look upon and be saved.

And as Moses lifted up the serpent in the wilderness, even so must the Son of man be lifted up. John 3:14-15

You can follow all the steps that have been laid out to shake off the snake, but without knowing the King of Kings, Jesus, you will never be free from the torment, the guilt, or the shame. Place your life, again, firmly in the hands of Jesus and be liberated. For whom the son sets free is free indeed. Free from condemnation, free from frustration, and free to overcome anything the enemy brings your way.

**Beloved, think it not strange concerning the fiery trial which is to try you, as though some strange thing happened unto you: But rejoice, inasmuch as ye are partakers of Christ's sufferings; that, when his glory shall be revealed, ye may be glad also with exceeding joy.
I Peter 4:12-13**

PRAYER OF SALVATION

If you read this book and are struggling with frustration, anxiety, adversity or fear and have not made Jesus the Lord of Your Life you have missed out on the ultimate message of Salvation. Don't attempt to overcome it on your own. Jesus is here for you with outstretched arms waiting for you to cry out to HIM for help. Do It Now and Be Saved. Pray this prayer where you are and believe it with all your heart.

Lord Jesus, Forgive me for going it alone, without you. I recognize today I do need a savior. I believe you died for me and rose again to show me the way to the Father. Now by an act of my will I ask you Jesus, Come Into My heart, Be My Savior and Lord. I want to follow You for the rest of my Life and I'll Never turn back. Heal me , cleanse me, and make me whole. In Jesus Name. Amen.

ABOUT THE BACK COVER

Professional and patient centered health organizations (such as The World Health Organization) use the traditional symbol of medicine, the staff of Asclepius with a single serpent encircling a staff. It is classically depicted as a rough-hewn knotty tree limb. Asclepius was an ancient Greek physician who was deified in Greek Mythology as the god of medicine. He is usually shown as a bearded man wearing a robe with his chest uncovered and holding a staff. The single serpent coiled around it is meant to symbolize renewal of youth as the serpent casts off its skin.

After Moses lifted up the fiery serpent in the wilderness and the Israelites looked upon it and received their healing (see Numbers 21) it became a practice by some to make idols depicting the raised up snake. Years later, as documented in II Kings 8:14, King Hezekiah boldly responded to such idolatry and tore down the brazen image of the snake made by Moses, known as Nehushtan, because people were worshipping and burning incense to it.

As a christian physician I prefer to view this traditional medical symbol as being more closely related to the biblical representation from Numbers rather than that of Greek mythological lore. In either case, however, it is important that we understand no matter how holy or intriguing the origins of any symbol, *no* icon is ever meant to, nor should be used to replace the real savior. Their only purpose is to direct our gaze toward Jesus and our worship is meant to be reserved for him alone.

A.J. RUBANO, D.C.

A.J. Rubano D.C. was born in Lakewood, New Jersey. He attended Rutgers University in New Brunswick, N.J. and Life Chiropractic College in Marietta, Ga. where he received a doctorate in chiropractic medicine. He is a licensed Chiropractor in Florida and New Jersey with a focus on accident and disc related injuries.

Dr. Rubano has been married to his wife, Sonia, for nineteen years. They have three children; Kyra, Philip, and Kayla.

To have Dr. A.J. hold a health seminar at your church or town, for other speaking engagements, or if you would like more information about the products and services he offers you may contact:

A.J. Rubano, D.C.
C/o Accurate Chiropractic LLC
Fort Myers, FL 33908
(239)481-8811
Dr. Rubano's website is www.diskease.com

LaVergne, TN USA
22 January 2011
213509LV00001B/4/P